Everyday Life in the Classic Maya World

Everyday Life in the Classic Maya World introduces readers to a range of people who lived during the Classic period (200–800 CE) of Maya civilization. Traci Ardren here reconstructs the individual experiences of Maya people across all social arenas and experiences, including less-studied populations, such as elders, children, and non-gender binary people. Putting people, rather than objects, at the heart of her narrative, she examines the daily activities of a small rural household of farmers and artists, hunting and bee-keeping rituals, and the bustling activities of the urban marketplace. Ardren bases her study on up-to-date and diverse sources and approaches, including archaeology, art history, epigraphy, and ethnography. Her volume reveals the stories of ancient Maya people and also shows the relevance of those stories today.

Written in an engaging style, *Everyday Life in the Classic Maya World* offers readers at all levels a view into the amazing accomplishments of a culture that continues to fascinate.

Traci Ardren is Professor of Anthropology at the University of Miami. Her research has been supported by the National Geographic Society and the National Science Foundation. She is the author of *Social Identities in the Classic Maya Northern Lowlands: Gender, Age, Memory, and Place* (University of Texas Press, 2015), editor of *Her Cup for Sweet Cacao: Food in Ancient Maya Society* (University of Texas Press, 2020), and coeditor of *The Maya World* (Routledge, 2020).

Everyday Life in the Classic Maya World

TRACI ARDREN
University of Miami

CAMBRIDGE
UNIVERSITY PRESS

Shaftesbury Road, Cambridge CB2 8EA, United Kingdom

One Liberty Plaza, 20th Floor, New York, NY 10006, USA

477 Williamstown Road, Port Melbourne, VIC 3207, Australia

314–321, 3rd Floor, Plot 3, Splendor Forum, Jasola District Centre,
New Delhi – 110025, India

103 Penang Road, #05–06/07, Visioncrest Commercial, Singapore 238467

Cambridge University Press is part of Cambridge University Press & Assessment, a department of the University of Cambridge.

We share the University's mission to contribute to society through the pursuit of education, learning and research at the highest international levels of excellence.

www.cambridge.org
Information on this title: www.cambridge.org/9781107040670

DOI: 10.1017/9781139629232

© Traci Ardren 2023

This publication is in copyright. Subject to statutory exception and to the provisions of relevant collective licensing agreements, no reproduction of any part may take place without the written permission of Cambridge University Press & Assessment.

First published 2023

Printed in the United Kingdom by TJ Books Limited, Padstow Cornwall

A catalogue record for this publication is available from the British Library.

Library of Congress Cataloging-in-Publication Data
NAMES: Ardren, Traci, author.
TITLE: Everyday life in the classic Maya world / Tracy Ardren, University of Miami.
DESCRIPTION: Cambridge ; New York, NY : Cambridge University Press, 2023. | Includes bibliographical references.
IDENTIFIERS: LCCN 2022049598 (print) | LCCN 2022049599 (ebook) |
ISBN 9781107040670 (hardback) | ISBN 9781107682917 (paperback) |
ISBN 9781139629232 (epub)
SUBJECTS: LCSH: Mayas–Social life and customs. | Mayas–Civilization.
CLASSIFICATION: LCC F1435.3.S7 A73 2023 (print) | LCC F1435.3.S7 (ebook) |
DDC 305.897/42–dc23/eng/20221214
LC record available at https://lccn.loc.gov/2022049598
LC ebook record available at https://lccn.loc.gov/2022049599

ISBN 978-1-107-04067-0 Hardback
ISBN 978-1-107-68291-7 Paperback

Cambridge University Press & Assessment has no responsibility for the persistence or accuracy of URLs for external or third-party internet websites referred to in this publication and does not guarantee that any content on such websites is, or will remain, accurate or appropriate.

For Anthony P. Andrews

in celebration of forty years of teaching – thank you for opening a door to the Maya world for me and so many others

Contents

List of Figures and Maps	*page* ix
Acknowledgments	xi
1 Introduction	1
Nature of the Data	2
Environmental Factors	7
Chronology, Political Systems, and Modern Maya People	12
Cosmology	15
How This Book Is Organized	20
2 The Domestic World	24
The Morning Meal	25
Craft Activities	34
The Evening and Leisure	40
3 Fields and Forests	46
People of Maize (and Other Foods Too)	47
Apiculture	56
The Forest	59
Caves and Cave Ritual	63
4 Into the City	69
An Urban Landscape	70
Literacy	80
Ball Games and Royal Responsibility	85

5	Palace Life	94
	Spiritual Mediation	95
	Diplomacy	104
	Courtly Arts	112
6	To the Coast	124
	Traveling to the Sea	125
	Coastal Activities	133
	Traders and Their Goods	137
7	Conclusion	147
	After the Classic Period	148
	Modern Maya Perspectives on Their Classic Heritage	157
Bibliography		163
Index		169

Figures and Maps

1.1 Wealthy merchant known as the "Woman in Blue," from a Classic period mural, Calakmul, Mexico *page* 3
1.2 The author excavating ceramic vessels from a burial context at Xuenkal, Mexico 6
1.3 Map of the Maya area 8
1.4 Agua Volcano, near Antigua, Guatemala 9
1.5 Rainforest meets the Gulf of Mexico 10
1.6 Usumacinta River canyon 10
1.7 Cenote Ik Kil, near Valladolid, Mexico 11
1.8 Cache offering from Caracol, Belize 17
1.9 The Cross Group at Palenque, Mexico 19
2.1 Grinding stone for processing maize, Chunchucmil, Mexico 26
2.2 Young Maya women visit as they gather water in ceramic jars at a well in Yucatan, Mexico, circa 1945 28
2.3 Classic period ceramic vase of supernatural deer in conversation with an Old God of the underworld 30
2.4 *Ceiba speciosa*, the sacred tree of the ancient Maya 32
2.5 Domestic burial of an ancestor with ceramic vessels and shell offerings, Xuenkal, Mexico 34
2.6 Elaborate "eccentric" flint ornament 36
2.7 Modern Tzeltal Maya potter in the highlands of Guatemala using a traditional methodology 39
3.1 Juun Ixim, the Maize Deity, from a carved vase found in a burial at Xuenkal, Mexico 48

ix

3.2	Yearbearer ceremonies in the Dresden Codex showing offerings from the cardinal directions	51
3.3	The Three Sisters growing together in Yucatan, Mexico	54
3.4	Xunan Kab native Maya stingless bees kept in a hollow log in Yaxunah, Yucatan, Mexico	58
3.5	Hunter with blade-tipped spear on a Classic period ceramic vase	62
3.6	Cave with collapsed roof, Yucatan, Mexico.	64
3.7	Balancanche Cave, Yucatan, Mexico	66
4.1	Lidar imagery of the ancient lakeside city of Coba, Quintana Roo, Mexico	71
4.2	Map of central La Corona, Guatemala.	72
4.3	View of the nearby lake system from the top of the tallest pyramid at Coba	78
4.4	Examples of six different methods available to write the ajaw title during the Classic period	81
4.5	Monkey god of writing, patron of artists on a Classic period ceramic vase	82
4.6	Ceramic figurine of a warrior with shield and skull necklace	87
4.7	Ball game yoke, or belt, made of polished limestone	90
4.8	Ballplayers in traditional uniform engaged in play	91
5.1	Classic Codex-style vessel with three wahy spirits	96
5.2	Carved wooden deity figure	98
5.3	Portrait of Lady K'awiil Ajaw	100
5.4	Two royal lords visiting in a palace	108
5.5	Portrait of a lord	114
5.6	Classic period ceramic figurine and rattle	116
5.7	Example of graffiti, Tikal, Guatemala	119
6.1	Rollout photograph of the Star Wars Vase	126
6.2	Muyil Structure 1	129
6.3	The Caribbean coast at Muyil, Mexico	130
6.4	Stela depicting a Classic Maya fisherman	133
6.5	God L depicted on a carved ceramic vessel from Chunchucmil, Mexico	139
6.6	Classic Maya vase depicting traders presenting cotton to a lord	140
6.7	Royal earflare carved from spiny bivalve, or spondylus shell, Yaxuna	144
6.8	Carved ear ornaments	146

Acknowledgments

A great number of colleagues have shared their data and ideas with me in the course of writing this book. I thank you all and hope to repay your generosity in the future. Many long-term collaborative relationships improve my scholarship and inspire me to ask even more interesting questions. For hours of conversation and debate I thank Alejandra Alonso Olvera, Anthony P. Andrews, George J. Bey III, John F. Chuchiak, Michael D. Coe, David Freidel, Scott R. Hutson, Matthew Restall, William Ringle, Amara Solari, Travis W. Stanton, and Gabrielle Vail. I thank those whom I have had the privilege to teach and now call colleagues for their contributions to the ideas presented here, especially Tanya Anaya, Chelsea Blackmore, Ryan H. Collins, Harper Dine, Chelsea Fisher, Nelda Issa, Justin P. Lowry, Steph Miller, Horvey Palacios, Patrick Rohrer, Trent Stockton, Daniel Vallejo Váliz, and Julie K. Wesp. Colleagues who shared ideas, images, or citations are too numerous to name, but at great risk I will try by thanking Adolfo Ivan Batun Alpuche, Marcello A. Canuto, Nicolas P. Carter, Arlen F. Chase, Tracy Devine-Guzman, Viviana Diaz-Balsera, Jerald Ek, Karen Elwell, Ashuni Erb, Lilia Fernandez Souza, Fernando Godos, Stanley Guetner, Stephen D. Houston, Maxime Lamoureux St-Hilaire, Victoria Lyall, Aline Magnoni, Simon Martin, Mallory E. Matsumoto, Shankari Patel, Dominique Rissolo, Donald A. Slater, Vera Tiesler, Walter Witschey, and Marc Zender. A very special thanks to Patricia A. McAnany for asking to hear my voice.

At the University of Miami I thank Leonidas Bachas, Dean of the College of Arts and Sciences, for allowing me to take the time to finish this manuscript; Caleb Everett, former Chair of the Department of Anthropology, for his enthusiasm about the project; Arthur Dunkleman, Jose Miguel Cabrera, and Gisele Rocha of the Kislak

Collection at Richter Library Special Collections; and Jill Deupi, Director of the Lowe Art Museum, for permission to reproduce images from University of Miami collections. For additional images I thank most sincerely Victoria Lyall at the Denver Museum of Art, the Dumbarton Oaks Research Library and Collection, Lic. María del Perpetuo Soccoro Villarreal Escárrega, Coodinadora Nacional de Conservación del Patrimonio Cultural, Instituto Nacional de Antropología e Historia, the Peabody Museum of Archaeology and Ethnology, the University of Pennsylvania Museum of Archaeology and Anthropology, and especially the generous assistance of Justin P. Lowry. Finally, with deep appreciation I thank Beatrice Rehl and her staff at the Cambridge University Press for their patience and unflagging support.

1

Introduction

Why do the ancient Maya fascinate us so much? The field of Maya studies is filled with stories of a single site visit or artwork that changed the course of someone's life – suddenly we must know all we can about this very foreign culture located so close to home. There are scores of Maya conferences open to the public, and magazines like *National Geographic* or *Archaeology* seem to run a story about the ancient Maya in nearly every other issue. Is it because they are mysterious and unknown? Or because they mastered a challenging tropical environment for over a thousand years? Is it that many Americans travel to Mexico and become familiar, even if only in a passing sense, with the deep history of Indigenous Mexico? Or is it simply the superb artwork and architecture of Classic Maya culture, with its graceful lines and intricate stonework? This book sets out to introduce the new student or admirer of ancient Maya society to the best approximation that current scholarship has to offer of the glorious achievements and challenges of this unique ancient society. To those who have already visited the ancient cities of the Maya scattered throughout southern Mexico, Guatemala, Belize, and Honduras, this book will help the reader see the people who populated those wonderfully diverse and complex cities, and the countryside in between. To those who are new to this culture, I hope to share some of the excitement scholars like myself have for the rich history of Maya society, and to bring you a few steps closer to what life was like in ancient Maya times.

NATURE OF THE DATA

If you know anything about the ancient Maya you likely know that archaeologists are very fond of excavating the ancient tombs of Maya kings and queens. Every few years a new undisturbed Maya tomb with all its riches is opened from deep within a pyramid. These discoveries remind us of the sense of wonder we had as children, when the world was filled with unknown treasures from days gone by. Because the ancient Maya had a strong belief in the afterlife, like Pharaonic Egyptians they filled a royal burial with all that a royal ruler would need in the underworld – things such as ritual tools, delicious food and drink, and elaborate jewelry befitting their status – many of which were made by expert craftspeople and today are justly considered masterpieces of art. In the later chapters of this book we will explore what daily life was like for the royalty, or the ruling families, and those who surrounded them to perform courtly activities. Their palace life was filled with intrigue, luxury, and dynastic competition much as the lives of Medieval European royalty or Chinese dynastic royalty. These people created the only system of full literacy in the ancient New World, and used these hieroglyphs to commemorate their accomplishments in books and carved stone. The writing and calendrical systems of the ancient Maya are unsurpassed in ancient New World history, and the Maya are one of a handful of ancient cultures that created a fully phonetic written language like our own. Why wouldn't these accomplishments fascinate us?

But in order for those elites to have time to learn how to read and write hieroglyphs, many, many other people had to grow the food they ate, weave fabric for their clothing, build palaces and patios where they lived, and defend their cities from often aggressive neighbors. Fortunately, in addition to excavating ancient Maya tombs, the field of Maya studies is rich in data on all these other people as well, often labeled "commoners," and described as the vast and diverse bulk of Maya society who were not discussed in writing and had less access to resources and state power. This book will try to bring them to life also, and to show how the life of a humble farmer was interconnected with the lives of the royalty that appear much more frequently in popular media. Increasingly, we are able to discern more about the lives of the vast middle of Maya society: the bureaucrats, administrators,

Introduction 3

FIGURE 1.1 Wealthy merchant known as the "Woman in Blue," from a Classic period mural on the Chiik Nahb structure sub 1-4, Calakmul, Mexico. Photograph courtesy of Proyecto de Conservación y Estudio del Conjunto Pictórico Chiik Nahb, Acrópolis Norte, Calakmul. Coordinación Nacional de Conservación del Patrimonio Cultural del Instituto Nacional de Antropología e Historia de México. Photo by Marcos Deli and photo mosaic by Diego Ángeles.

merchants, skilled tradespeople, architects, and healers – those who were neither royalty nor commoners (Figure 1.1). Scholars are slow to adjust their models of ancient societies, but today we acknowledge the importance of moving beyond a binary of inequality that includes only the nobles and the poor. One useful suggestion is that we relinquish "elite" and "commoner" in favor of more specific terms such as the occupational categories listed above, which better capture systematic measures of wealth, status, and power.[1]

Maya studies has a vast assortment of data available, because the ancient Maya not only left written records and pyramids; they left material evidence and art that speaks to every aspect of ancient lives. We can excavate the gardens where they grew papaya and chili peppers and find evidence of those plants in the soil. Animal bones left over from daily meals and ceremonial feasts can be identified to help us know how they hunted, what they ate, and what foods held ritual significance. While royals went into death accompanied by a

[1] Hutson 2020:407–423.

rich assortment of their favorite items, ancient Maya people of all social levels wore their favorite jewelry when they were buried. Often their families sent them into the afterlife with a ceramic plate or obsidian blade that helps us understand how their identity was symbolized by the tools they used every day. Archaeologists study the homes of farmers and merchants of all social levels to see how their living environment differed from (or was similar to) the lives of the elite. Art historians look for patterns in figurines found in the homes of nearly all ancient Maya people just as often as they look for patterns in elite portraiture. Epigraphers decipher hieroglyphic inscriptions and help us understand who was literate and who was not, as well as how those who held political power used writing to uphold that power. Ethnohistorians translate documents written in Maya languages from the period when Europeans first arrived in this part of the world and show how Maya people quickly adapted to new systems of authority as well as how they resisted or embraced Spanish culture. Finally, we are truly fortunate that today in Mexico, Guatemala, Belize, and Honduras, millions of people speak Mayan languages and keep Maya cultural practices alive in their own 21st-century way. These modern Maya people are not a uniform culture by any means, and there are thrilling differences between what a person who speaks Maya as their native language in rural Belize or the modern city of Merida thinks, believes, and knows about Maya history. But our understanding of ancient Maya life is undoubtedly much richer because certain elements of modern Maya life, such as the value placed on corn in the diet and as a ritual food, the importance of gender-specific work in the household but also in factories or hotels, and the value of learning and speaking Mayan languages, persist today.

These manifold data speak to different ancient lives and tell different stories about the ancient people who lived in the Maya area during the Classic period (200–800 CE). For the most part hieroglyphic inscriptions and texts concern the lives of the "1 percent" – the most powerful and privileged members of society, who were fully literate and controlled tightly their access to the historical record. These texts were written for posterity, for other members of the 1 percent, and as magical incantations to attempt to control the weather, land, deities, and fortunes of each polity or dynastically ruled city-state. Art history tells us stories of the elite as well, as they controlled the production of

Introduction

the most elaborate and formal artistic works, but art was not only the province of the wealthy. Even members of modest households made clay figurines and personal ornaments, and there are wonderful stories hidden in crafts, such as pottery and cloth, that were made in every household. In Maya studies archaeology is the great democratizer, and the techniques of archaeological research can speak to all members of ancient Maya society, although scholars today acknowledge we have often overlooked certain populations like women, children, or elders, due to our own cultural prejudices. In short, there are many stories to tell about daily life in ancient Maya society, and no one book or analytical technique can hope to capture them all. However, by utilizing current data as skillfully as possible, and acknowledging that we do not have enough information on certain understudied groups, this volume attempts to convey a wide swath of the astounding stories available to us today about ancient Maya people. Their lives were rich and complex, full of happiness as well as stress. Some had vast material advantages over others, while some had greater freedom of movement and self-determination. This volume seeks to bring the reader closer to the actual experiences of living in Classic Maya culture by emphasizing the human experiences to which we all are subject, whether we live in an ancient city carved out of the tropical jungle or a small apartment in a contemporary urban jungle. It is not an act of fantasy to try to blur the distinctions between present and past – it can be an exercise in appreciating the common experiences all humans share while learning from the great accomplishments and failures of societies just as elaborate as our own.

The book you are reading is also shaped by my own experiences and life story. I have directed archaeological excavations in the Maya area for over thirty years, and collaborated with Yucatec Maya speakers from Yaxunah, Mexico, for most of that time (Figure 1.2). I was trained by archaeologists who worked closely with art historians and museum professionals because they had an appreciation for how profoundly art speaks to Maya cultural values. I was fortunate to have an undergraduate professor who grew up in Mexico and spent his career working at Maya cities of the Yucatan, a strong influence on my choice to center my research in the northern Maya lowlands. I am a white cis-gendered woman from a middle-class family who spent their discretionary funds on travel and would probably describe themselves

FIGURE 1.2 The author excavating ceramic vessels from a burial context at Xuenkal, Mexico. Photograph courtesy of the Proyecto Arqueologico Xuenkal.

as animists, taking spiritual lessons from nature. My archaeological research in the Maya area continued while I had two sons, and they accompanied me to the field. I improvised how to balance field research and parenting, and we experienced the extraordinary kindness of many Maya people and Mayanist scholars who rescued me from my improvisations. I have written about how taking my kids into the field transformed my understanding of modern Maya life, as once I had kids, Maya women felt we had a lot more in common and started talking to me about their lives. I am fortunate to teach at a university and my choices about what to include in this volume are shaped by the decades of students I have taught about the Maya and their questions about this amazing culture. I am also deeply committed to sharing the knowledge my field produces with the interested public, and through museum exhibits, public lectures, and articles I have developed a sense of what questions visitors to the Maya area ask the most. Everything I have to say about the ancient Maya is shaped by my friends and colleagues in Yaxunah.

Scholars make choices about what data to utilize – even social scientists who follow the scientific method of hypothesis testing – and I consider myself one of those scientists, gravitate toward certain questions or aspects of ancient cultures. This book is the result of a conversation between my particular research interests and experiences alongside what my students and friends have wanted to know about the ancient Maya that draws on the latest and best scholarly research. I say all this to demystify the process by which archaeologists and other scholars create the depictions of ancient societies we put out into the world. My story is not the only story about ancient Maya lives and I embrace that fact.

ENVIRONMENTAL FACTORS

You also might know that the ancient Maya lived in the tropical rainforests, where thick vines cover pyramids and wild jaguars roam the cities. This is partly true. Another well-earned fascination with the Maya stems from their success in a challenging tropical environment. Long ago, archaeologists and other scholars of ancient history thought a complex state could not succeed in the tropical regions of the world. This misconception was based on incomplete information about the stunning accomplishments of ancient people in the tropics of Southeast Asia, the Amazon, and Mesoamerica, the area from Mexico south through Central America. Yet living in the tropics does pose many challenges, especially to a complex state facing issues such as food storage, maintenance of infrastructure, and widespread agriculture. We are still discovering how the ancient Maya managed their environments, or how they were managed by them – but by any measure it is certainly an impressive story. The Maya region is usually defined as southern Mexico: the modern states of Chiapas, Campeche, Yucatan, and Quintana Roo that make up the Yucatan peninsula; all of Guatemala and Belize; and northern Honduras (Figure 1.3). This is a large area that was never brought under a single authority but where cultural traits are shared in a patchwork of independent but allied city-states. Within this area there are both highlands that run parallel to the Pacific Coast and stretch into lower

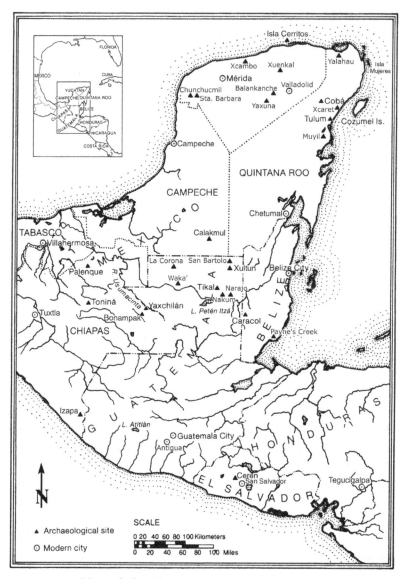

FIGURE 1.3 Map of the Maya area, showing archaeological sites and modern cities mentioned in the text. Illustration by the author and Michael C. Owens.

Introduction   9

FIGURE 1.4 Agua Volcano, near Antigua, Guatemala, in the Maya highlands. Volcanic activity created the abundant obsidian resources used by ancient Maya people, but remains a risk to modern occupants of the Maya highlands. Photo: Dave Wilson, WebArtz Photography / Moment / Getty Images.

Guatemala, and lowlands that run from where the highlands end up through the tip of the Yucatan peninsula. Resources and terrain vary in predictable ways between the highlands and the lowlands, with granite, obsidian, and jade found in the mountainous region, while tropical animals and plants are found in the lowlands (Figure 1.4). Add to this the longest coastline of any ancient society, with approximately 1,500 kilometers of inlets, bays, and shallow beaches. Coastal resources such as shell and dried fish made their way deep inland throughout almost the entire Maya area (Figure 1.5). In the middle of the peninsula, the lowlands are cut through with rivers that often run over dangerous rapids or through narrow gorges that made the ancient cities perched on nearby escarpments easy to defend (Figure 1.6). Toward the northern part of the peninsula the rivers disappear but are replaced by natural sinkholes that provide access to underground freshwater reservoirs (Figure 1.7). The seasons in the entire Maya area, as in most tropical regions, are governed by the presence or absence of daily rains. In the summer it often rains every

FIGURE 1.5 Rainforest meets the Gulf of Mexico along the western coast of the Yucatan peninsula, Bay of Campeche. Photo: Cavan Images/ Cavan / Getty Images.

FIGURE 1.6 Usumacinta River canyon, the border between Guatemala and Mexico. Photo: Kenneth Garreth, Danita Delamont/ Alamy Stock Photo.

Introduction

FIGURE 1.7   Cenote Ik Kil, near Valladolid, Mexico. Photo: Wendy White / Alamy Stock Photo.

day and powerful storms or hurricanes blow through the region. In the winter it is drier and it rains less frequently.

Maize, or what North Americans call corn, was domesticated in the dry highlands of central Mexico thousands of years before Maya centers emerged. Scholars agree maize agriculture was already widely practiced by the time of the first Maya rulers. But agriculture in a tropical zone is fraught with risks – pests, droughts, and storms are more common than they are in temperate highland climates. Because ancient Maya society was completely dependent on maize agriculture, the arrival of daily rains at a predictable time of the year so seeds could sprout and crops ripen, was a huge preoccupation in Classic Maya culture. Maya royalty portrayed themselves in elite art dressed as the Maize Deity, a beautiful, youthful, gender-fluid figure that embodied the potential of a young maize plant. Rituals were performed in urban centers to call in the power of the mighty storm god Chac, when maize fields needed moisture. Temples were decorated with images of a native honeybee deity who helped pollinate the cornfields. Many of the major deities of Maya culture corresponded to aspects of the natural world that facilitated the growth of maize. But the lowlands in particular provide a wealth of other foods to feed the large urban populations of Maya cities. In addition to corn, which was planted by hand with beans and squash, Maya people domesticated the turkey and duck for food and hunted deer, peccary, iguana, turtle, and fish to round out their meals. Native fruit such as papaya, guava, and avocado added calories and flavor to the Maya diet, and nearly every household grew vegetables and herbs such as chili peppers, bush spinach, and cucumber. The wetter regions of the Maya area were conducive to growing cacao, or chocolate, and even modest households in places like the river valleys of Belize had cacao on hand.[2] The vanilla orchid is also native to the Maya area and likely was added to cacao drinks, along with chili powder and/or honey.

CHRONOLOGY, POLITICAL SYSTEMS, AND MODERN MAYA PEOPLE

No matter how much you know about the ancient Maya you might be a little uncertain about whether or not they were living in cities when the Spanish arrived in the 16th-century New World. This uncertainty is understandable because the great encounters between kings of the Indigenous states in the New World and Spanish conquistadors are well known and shape how we think about the ancient history of the Americas. In the case of the ancient Maya, the story is a little more complex, and while Maya people certainly met Cortes and probably even Columbus when Europeans first traveled into Mexican waters, the elaborate Maya cities discussed in this book were not occupied when those meetings occurred. The chronology of ancient Maya culture is centered around their urban florescence – a word that was used by early Mayanists, or scholars of the Maya, to describe what they saw as the most interesting period of Maya history. Today we generally stick to slightly more neutral periodization terms, and organize Maya history into the Preclassic (also still called the Formative period by some scholars, 800 BCE–200 CE), the Classic (200–800 CE), the Terminal Classic (800–1100 CE), and the Postclassic (1100–1521 CE). The Preclassic period sets the stage for the urban explosion of

---

[2] McAnany and Murata 2006.

the Classic, but also for the emergence of endemic or entrenched social stratification, the separation of farmers from rulers, and all the associated hierarchy that made the state-level social organization of the Classic period possible. During the Preclassic period Maya people transitioned from living in small egalitarian settlements to building the largest stucco-covered pyramids of their entire history. Shamans and healers evolve into royal kings and queens, and dynasties are founded that last for over 500 years, well into the Classic period. The writing system is codified, and images of divine rulers become standardized across the Maya area. It is a time of tremendous innovation and expansion.

These accomplishments provide the foundation of the Classic period, when Maya culture becomes the familiar ancient state often depicted in popular media. Most Maya art in museums around the word originated at the hands of artists working during the Classic period, when there were thousands of Maya cities each filled with thousands of people. Semi-divine dynastic rule was well established and nearly all ruling families were allied with one of a few large and powerful sovereign lines. Rural farmers had the responsibility of providing food for urban elites, and markets emerged for the exchange of commodities as well as exotic trade items. Alliances based on tenuous claims to kinship kept the lower social ranks indebted to the elites, who were understood to have divine or holy blood running through their veins. Large rituals in urban centers kept the majority of the population invested in their system of governance, although those who did not have faith were free to leave the cities and settle somewhere quieter. Competition for territory to support such an administrative burden was fierce, and boundary warfare became a constant feature of life. After six centuries the infrastructure that made the Classic period possible started to fray – the delicate tropical environment was overtaxed, the cities were full of too many people living too closely together, and unending wars had taken a toll on the population. We call this period the Terminal Classic. This ominous term attempts to capture some of the social changes underway in the 300-year period when the Maya state as it was known in the Classic period began to fail in a systematic way. Our first clue to the changes that took place in the Terminal Classic period was the evidence that many cities in the southern lowlands were abandoned at this time – or at least there was no new construction or inscriptions, and existing infrastructure was no longer maintained. Some scholars call this the Maya Collapse, although since we know Maya people lived on for many centuries, and survive today, it was really just a collapse of their Classic period political structure, not of the culture as a whole. "Postclassic" might sound like everything that happened after the party was over, but in fact this was another hugely dynamic period when almost everything changed and Maya people reinvented their society yet again. The Postclassic Maya era is contemporary with the rise of the Aztec Empire, which had a profound impact from the US Southwest all the way down into lower Central America. But the changes that define the Postclassic Maya period were not due to Aztec influence but rather were Maya responses to challenges and opportunities in their own area. Urban cities had largely failed and the population moved back to smaller, more sustainable settlements. The few cities that flourished did so due to impressive trade connections that brought goods and ideas together from throughout Mesoamerica. Art changed to reflect ideas and themes common throughout the region from which exotic trade goods flowed. So while the Maya never disappeared, as popular media often suggest, they did abandon an urban way of life and probably lost faith in their semi-divine royalty, opting instead for an even more decentralized form of political autonomy and individual self-reliance. This resilience was needed again at the end of the Postclassic period when the Spanish arrived in the early 16th century seeking converts and gold. Despite a brutal 500 years of colonial occupation, Maya people survived as many other New World Indigenous people did, by removing themselves from contact with the strangers and living as deeply within the jungle as possible, far from Spanish settlements. They mounted resistance movements that drew large numbers of Indigenous people together, and they made alliances with foreign powers. Today there are 7 million Maya-speaking people in Mexico, Guatemala, Belize, and Honduras, with a diaspora that spreads throughout the United States and Canada. They are lawyers and politicians, professors and Nobel laureates, as well as subsistence farmers, weavers, and fisherfolk. Modern class differences influence how much modern Maya-speaking people know about their ancient ancestors, but Indigenous oral history and centuries of scientific research have demonstrated a clear line of cultural connection between the people who built the ancient cities in the jungle described in this book, and the modern people who farm, work, and govern the countries of the Maya region today. More and more Maya authors who write in one of the thirty modern Mayan languages, whether they are archaeologists, poets, or priests, are making their work available for Spanish or English readers curious about the ancient roots of this rich Indigenous culture.[3]

COSMOLOGY

Almost anyone who has visited Tulum, Antigua, or the other popular tourist destinations within the Maya world knows there was a large pantheon of Classic Maya deities. It can be confusing to try and learn their names and attributes, especially when these names vary in spelling and importance from region to region. Earlier scholars tried to organize the ancient Maya pantheon so that it corresponded to Western mythological systems like the ancient Greeks and Romans, but this was an artificial imposition on a very non-Western New World religious tradition. Today we understand that the best sources for learning how ancient Maya people thought about the universe is the evidence they left us in texts, ritual locations, and religious or mythological art. Ancient Maya art has helped us understand the belief system of Classic Maya people, and we are fortunate that Maya elites often commissioned artwork that depicted important mythological scenes. When we combine these sources with a 16th-century document that recorded, in K'iche' Maya language, a much earlier origin myth, we actually know quite a lot about the very complex religious ideology of ancient Maya culture.[4]

It is important to remember that like most non-Western cultures of the past and today, religion was not something easily separated from daily life in ancient Maya times. Small rituals permeated the chores and leisure activities of most people, and while there were certain full-time religious specialists at elite social levels, most people shared what we might today call religious or spiritual activities with their families and neighbors. The ancient Maya lived in an animistic world, meaning

[3] Cuevas Cob 1998; Ak'abal 1999; Frischmann and Villegas 2016.
[4] Chinchilla Mazariegos 2017.

that all entities, living (in the Western sense) and not, held soul force. A mountain held tremendous soul force, as much as or more than a divine king – but so did a tiny jade bead, wild monkey, or beehive. Certain substances had a particularly valued form of soul force, for example, jade, which the ancient Maya prized above gold or silver, and cacao or chocolate beans. These were substances that inherently embodied the divine, like the royalty who governed Maya cities. Much of ancient Maya ritual was concerned with the movement of soul force found in certain substances like royal blood, copal incense, or sacred animals, from humans to a deity or venerated ancestor. Offerings of these precious substances were made by the devout on calendrically important days like the beginning of a new year or the anniversary of a king's death, as well as when a special occasion demanded it such as in preparation for war or at the accession of a new queen (Figure 1.8).

Within this animate world, ancestors held tremendous influence. All ancient Maya people practiced some form of ancestral worship or veneration. Maya royalty would often commission long hieroglyphic texts that recounted their descent from a distinguished lineage founder or some other illustrious ancestor. Nonelite craftspeople and farmers maintained ancestral shrines near their homes where the cremated remains of ancestors could be interred and visited frequently, or they buried their beloved dead under the floor of their home in a family crypt that was used over and over again. These examples demonstrate that existence and agency did not end at physical death within the ancient Maya belief system, and the spirits of ancestors could be petitioned for assistance with earthly matters when necessary. Deities were also called upon and Maya royals often performed ceremonies where they attempted to embody the nature and appearance of a deity in order to bring themselves into contact with a particular soul force. Major Classic Maya deities will be discussed throughout the book as we touch on the areas of life they governed.

All Indigenous Mesoamerican peoples, including the ancient Aztecs, Maya, Zapotecs, and others, shared a broadly similar origin story about how the world came to be, how humans came to inhabit the world, and the relationship between humans and the rest of the natural world. In each specific culture the names of major heroes and deities changed, and there were regional differences in how the

Introduction

FIGURE 1.8 Cache offering of a complete spiny oyster shell with greenstone, both substances that contained exceptional life force to the ancient Maya. Structure A8, Caracol, Belize. Courtesy of Arlen and Diane Chase, the Caracol Archaeological Project.

story was told, but the overall perspective was one in which time is cyclical and creation arose from the unpredictable force of transformation. Creation did not happen once; it happened multiple times, and was not perfect. Deities sometimes acted in unison but more often they acted in opposition. Their actions appear in the mythological narratives as cautionary tales about the power of creative inspiration, conflict, and transformation. As in many mythological systems, Maya creation deities appear as a primordial creator couple who take female and male form, and who work in concert each with their own skills, to create living creatures. Gender was a primary way in which Maya people ordered the universe, explained difference, and structured production of goods, families, and rituals. Gender appears often in Maya mythology as a clue to the importance of an activity: creation occurs when both male and female are balanced and in cooperation, young corn plants are bigendered, and the Maya maize deity is likewise gender-fluid, incorporating a youthful beauty that is neither fully male nor female. Old male gods of the underworld trap young goddesses in Maya myths that reflect cultural values about the vitality and fertility of the earth during the rainy season. Gender was not a limiting factor in expressions of the divine, as it can be in modern Western belief systems, but rather an essential component of the natural and supernatural world that conveyed important information to humans about how the universe was kept in balance.

One way in which the Mesoamerican cyclical understanding of time appears in Maya belief is in the repeated patterns of creation and destruction of the world. In each iteration prior to the world we live in now, there were earlier races of humans, often of inferior quality. Animals were created first, then mud people, then wooden people, and each was destroyed due to their failure to correctly recognize and praise the gods. But each failure provided the impetus for a new creation of better and more successful creatures. This is a fundamental aspect of Mesoamerican belief – creation of the world and its creatures, just like the creation of a ceramic vessel or hieroglyphic text, was the result of constant experimentation, failure, and accumulated expertise. We see this process at work in the myths of the Hero Twins, supernatural brothers who, through their repeated adventures hunting and journeying to the underworld, defeat the demons that would prevent the sun and moon from rising and thus keep the universe moving in an orderly fashion.

Sculptures from the important Maya site of Palenque contain long hieroglyphic texts and images describing the origins of the world and many of its major components from a Maya perspective such as the sun, warfare, maize, and the deities that provided the dynasty of Palenque with supernatural sanction (Figure 1.9). A passage at the Temple of the Cross details the importance of solar rebirth accompanied by imagery of the sacred World Tree growing from a plate

Introduction

FIGURE 1.9 The Cross Group at Palenque, Mexico. The Temple of the Cross, the Temple of the Sun, and the Temple of the Foliated Cross all record cosmological information about the origin of the world. Photograph by the author.

marked with the sign for sun.[5] A nearby shrine known as the Temple of the Sun has imagery and text concerning sacred warfare, which we know was much more than warfare in terms of battles and weaponry (which were also important to Maya rulers, as we will see in Chapter 4). Warfare in this type of cosmological context was a metaphor for the cyclical processes of experimentation, failure, and eventual success described in the paragraph above. In the imagery of this shrine the Jaguar War God, who travels between the stars and the watery underworld, does battle in order to perpetuate creation. The final textual passage, found at the Temple of the Foliated Cross, is dedicated to the power of agriculture and the importance of water. Maize is shown growing from a mask that represents the cosmic sea and the text describes the birth of K'awiil, the god of lightning and dynastic power. From this one site, which admittedly has a very rich record concerning the origin of the world, we learn about the

[5] Stuart and Stuart 2008.

importance of natural phenomena like lightning and stars, how ancient Maya people took lessons from the observation of these natural phenomena, and the spiritual importance they placed on certain aspects of their lives such as agriculture and warfare.

Maya cities are often described as haphazard in design or lacking a central plan, and it is true that they were never aligned to a single grid or arranged in the form of a sacred template like other cities of the ancient world. But this does not mean they lack an ideological basis or sense of order. Many household groups are arranged with a family shrine on the eastern side of the patio area. Settlements are often in sight of a significant natural landmark such as a sacred cave, mountain, or water source. The north-south axis is important in the arrangement of many Maya urban centers, with funerary pyramids more commonly in the northern neighborhood. Many Maya cities had architecture that was designed around astronomical phenomena such as the solstices and equinoxes, so the elites who moved through those buildings would have access to the particular soul force of an orderly universe. Clear ideas about how space should be used pervade all aspects of ancient Maya settlements.

HOW THIS BOOK IS ORGANIZED

This book presents my best estimation of what life was like in and around a Classic Maya city, using up-to-date information from a wide variety of sources. It is not meant to be a reconstructed history of a single city, but I drew extensively on the research to date at the Classic center of Coba, located in modern Quintana Roo, Mexico, to provide a data-centered basis for this narrative. Coba experienced a sixty-year period in the 7th century under three to four rulers including a very powerful royal queen who epitomized the ideal divine ruler of Classic Maya culture. Queen K'awiil Ajaw governed for many decades and grew the territory of her polity through wars of expansion, perhaps including the construction of a 100-kilometer-long road. She commemorated her military successes on huge carved stone monuments that display her captives and demanded that her portraits include full military regalia. Her court patronized the arts and sciences, and during this reign Maya scribes created highly advanced calendrical and mathematical inscriptions as well as the longest known Maya text

Introduction

on a stela. Her city-state had 50,000–70,000 citizens during this time and was one of the largest Classic Maya cities of the 7th century. It has the greatest number of carved stelae of any city in the northern lowlands, some of the tallest pyramids, and an extensive network of roads and causeways. In short, it provides ample inspiration as well as archeological and artistic data for an exploration of the daily lives of all social levels in the ancient period.

I want to introduce you to not only Queen K'awiil Ajaw but also other people that might have lived in the ancient city and its environs, including nearby farming and coastal settlements. I chose to give them Maya names, and their portraits in this book are drawn from the very best information we have about what life was like for women, men, non–gender binary people, children, elders, royals, farmers, artists, and so many more. Some of my colleagues may find these passages too fictionalized, and I am sensitive to the criticism that it is very hard to recover scientific information about specific individuals in the past. But it is far from impossible. I believe it is respectful and important to tell the individual stories and experiences of the ancient people who created the archaeological record we study today. They were grandmothers, explorers, and teachers in their time – not just numbers in an archaeological report. I hope these passages help erase the arbitrary line modern Western minds have drawn between the past and present.

We begin by considering the daily lives of the people who made the life of this queen possible. The majority of ancient Maya people lived on the outskirts of the exciting and bustling cities, close to the agricultural fields and forests that they tended. The crops grown outside the city and in their domestic gardens fed their families and were paid in tribute to the palace to feed royal families as well. In Chapter 2 we discover how domestic life was filled with crafting, gardening, and leisure. We will explore how ancient Maya families prepared daily meals, the animals and plants they kept in nearby gardens, the crafts they made, and how they spent leisure time in the evenings in the absence of modern illumination. Chapter 3 moves out of the domestic world and into the fields and forests nearby. What activities filled the days of an ancient Maya farmer? What rituals accompanied working a field and tending crops? The cornfield, or milpa, of Maya farmers was ideologically very important in Maya culture, and in many ways it was a microcosm of the settlement as a whole. Equally important was the boundary between cornfield and forest, and we will look at forest hunting practices as well as beekeeping along field/forest boundaries. Caves were also a ubiquitous part of the landscape and certain caves were reserved for ritual activities, which we look at in detail.

We move into the city in Chapter 4 by walking along the many paths and roadways that connected rural or suburban settlements to the urban center. The environment changes as one moves away from the agricultural sector and into the city – but so does the architecture and the activities performed on a daily basis. In this chapter we look at many of the craft specialties that took place inside the urban zone, including the marketplace that drew people in from the surrounding region. The ball game took place in the cities and we explore what we know about how it was played and the consequences at stake. Classic Maya culture is often seen as an urban culture but it was the interplay between rural and urban that kept the state functioning. Chapter 5 delves into daily life in the palace: the diplomatic visits and accompanying feasts that occupied royals, the dedicated work of the scribes who kept track of calendrical movements and recorded the activities of the royal family. Palaces were staffed with many specialists who helped keep the kingdom running, and yet members of the royal family had certain obligations to protect the spiritual fortune of their dynasties due to their special birth. Unequal access and institutionalized privilege was fundamental to ancient Maya society and it impacted the daily experiences of the elites as much as it did the rest of the population. Finally in Chapter 6 we explore what it was like to travel to a small Maya city at the sea, a port engaged in long-distance trade to provide inland polities with all the exotic goods they craved. From isotopic analyses we know that coastal settlements were filled with people of all social levels, often refugees from distant inland regions that left such places perhaps because they found them too predictable or maybe because they craved the adventurous life of a trader. The sea held a special place in Maya cosmology, as the origin of Maya people and the home of departed spirits. Traders enjoyed special privileges due to their connection to the sea, and religious pilgrimage sites were located on islands. As strongly as Maya people valued corn agriculture as a basis for their economy, they also depended on maritime trade for a wide variety of goods and services provided by traders who moved along the endless coastline in huge wooden canoes.

There is no single story of daily life in Classic Maya society, just as we could not tell a single story that captures the diversity of experiences in modern London or Miami. But by looking at evidence from the smallest rural settlement to the most elaborate palace, and the activities that were conducted every day in homes, fields, along the coast, and in the marketplace, I hope to capture some of the rich variety of lives that archaeologists and other scholars of the past are privileged to encounter.

Suggested Readings

Coe, Michael D., and Stephen D. Houston 2015 *The Maya*. New York: Thames and Hudson.

Restall, Matthew, and Amara Solari 2020 *The Maya: A Very Short Introduction*. Oxford: Oxford University Press.

2

The Domestic World

Most ancient Maya people spent the majority of their lives in and around domestic settings. Activities and experiences that occurred here shaped not only what people did every day, but how they thought about themselves in many important ways. Even kings and queens, with their very different living quarters, had rituals they performed for their subjects that reenacted the daily habits of simple domestic compounds. Living structures varied according to one's access to resources: royal families lived in roomy palaces made of stone, with plaster- and mural-covered walls and a high, vaulted ceiling. These buildings were often situated on small hills or artificial platforms to catch the breeze and prevent flooding during tropical rains. Middle-society homes were set atop smaller platforms, and may have had a plaster floor, but the walls of these homes were made of wood and the roofs of thatch. The simplest homes were set on the bedrock or ground level, with a packed dirt floor, wooden walls, and a thatch roof. Ironically, the wooden homes had many advantages over stone palaces – they allowed for more light and air to circulate, making them drier and in some cases cooler, and the materials to construct or repair these simple homes were easily available in the wetlands or forest outside Maya cities. However, they were very vulnerable to fire, especially during the dry season when an attack of flaming arrows could easily set an entire neighborhood aflame. Surrounding the central palaces and temples of ancient Maya cities were thousands of domestic or residential compounds, clusters of small houses, patios, and gardens occupied by extended multigenerational families of parents, children, spouses, and grandparents. In the 16th century, Spanish cleric Bishop Diego de Landa recorded that the Maya people of Yucatan had a matrilocal marriage practice, meaning that young men would move into the residential compound of their wives, so it is likely that multiple generations of family members lived together for most of their lifetime. Many of the tasks that took place in a compound, such as tending small animals, weaving, or gardening, were made easier by the collective efforts of an extended group of relatives.

THE MORNING MEAL

The day would start before dawn in an ancient Maya domestic compound. A younger woman, maybe a teenager or a newly married woman, would rise earlier than everyone else to grind corn that had been soaking overnight. Mesoamerican peoples invented a process to create corn dough called nixtamal, from the Nahua word *nixtamalli* used in the Aztec region of central Mexico, and it is a process still in use today by rural Mesoamericans. This ingenious discovery softened the hard, dried kernels of corn and prepared them for grinding into masa, or soft corn dough. A bit of lime ash, made from powdered limestone and wood ash, was added to a large pot of dried corn to soak overnight in the kitchen area of domestic compounds. The alkaline properties of the lime ash loosened the hulls from the kernels to make grinding easier, but it also increased the nutritional content of the corn. The corn was ground with a mano and metate, a smooth roller stone to crush food against a flat oblong stone, respectively, into a paste that could be used to make tortillas, tamales, pozole, and a host of other corn-based foods that Maya people ate at every meal (Figure 2.1). In Coba, the setting that inspired this book, pozole, or a thick porridge of corn and water, was likely the most common breakfast food, perhaps supplemented with sweet black zapote fruit or spicy habanero chili peppers. Later in the Terminal Classic period the flat ceramic cooking pan known as a comal was introduced to the northern Maya lowlands from central Mexico, and the tortilla became the food of choice for all three daily meals.

Young women would wake from their sleeping mats on the floor of a small thatched hut. The majority of houses were made much as they

FIGURE 2.1 Grinding stone for processing maize, found in a kitchen area of the Lool domestic group at Chunchucmil, Mexico. The author's son Cyrus provides scale. Photograph by the author.

were until very recently in rural Yucatecan villages with a stone foundation and tamped earth floor. The surface of the floor is made of a powdery form of limestone that becomes harder and harder with time and daily sweeping. Some ancient homes had a real plaster floor, which was easier to keep clean but required more resources to manufacture. Sleeping mats were made of woven palm fronds or other plant material, perhaps with a cotton pad, although cotton was a precious commodity largely monopolized by elites. The walls of the house were made of wooden poles lashed together with agave twine. These materials were easily obtained in the forest outside the city and could be quickly replaced when damaged. They allowed air to circulate through the house, which helped keep the home a cool and comfortable place to work. In the coldest time of the year, however, damp breezes entered at night and people would have to sleep next to one another for warmth.

Once everyone was awake, the floor of the house became a working area and sleeping mats were rolled up and put away. Children, small animals, and adults came and went throughout the interior of the house on their way to larger and more spacious outdoor patios and gardens. Sharp tools such as obsidian blades were stored in the rafters of the thatched roof, out of the way of children. Cooking fires were often located outside the home, where food could be prepared without causing smoke and heat to fill up the small house. Cooking fires were also a threat to thatch roofs that, once dry, were easily ignited by a stray spark. The fire was formed by three large stones with tinder placed between them. This "three-stone hearth" was ubiquitous in ancient Maya households and symbolized not only the place were nourishment was created but the symbolic heart of the home, the axis mundi or cosmic center point around which all productive activities revolved. The idea of the three-stone hearth was so important to the Maya that they had a constellation named for it, and kings and queens were buried with three jade beads in an elite version of this same idea. Rulers knew the importance of the three-stone hearth to Maya culture but they had access to the precious material jade that reinforced their importance as the leaders of Maya society.

Once corn masa was prepared, water also had to be brought from a nearby well. Large ancient Maya cities had many wells located in different neighborhoods, and in Coba, water was relatively easy to obtain as the limestone bedrock is soft and freshwater rivers travel underground through channels in the karst limestone. Young women or girls would ask to be sent to fetch water, filling huge ceramic jars they could balance on their heads as they walked slowly back to their homes (Figure 2.2). Fetching drinking water was an opportunity to visit with your friends, to walk side by side to the well and catch up on news from each other's households. The large jars were left in a shady part of the home, where the porous ceramic material allowed for a slow evaporation of moisture that kept the water cool all day, no matter how hot the weather. Maya cities had wells for drinking water

FIGURE 2.2 Young Maya women visit as they gather water in ceramic jars at a well in Yucatan, Mexico, circa 1945. Photo of historic postcard courtesy of Karen Elwell.

and others that were used only for ceremonial purposes, such as retrieving clean water for making balche, a mildly alcoholic mead that was used in many ceremonies and as an offering to deities. There were secret wells that only certain priests and priestesses used and others that were centrally located. On unlucky days the heavy water jar might break when someone tried to lift it and leave fragments for archaeologists to find today.

While girls were sent to fetch water, other members of the domestic compound would help tend to small animals kept in the yard outside their homes. Ancient Maya people domesticated the turkey and Muscovy duck, both hearty animals that provided tasty sources of meat and helped keep domestic gardens free of insects. They were allowed to roam freely between houses as both turkeys and ducks return to their roost at night. Some families kept so many ducks or turkeys that they built wicker enclosures for them. These circular pens had a stone foundation and the pen itself was made of perishable tree branches. There is also good evidence that ancient Maya people kept deer in their household gardens, or at least allowed deer to forage on the plants grown there. Deer meat was highly prized in ancient Maya cuisine and may have been turned over to the queen or king by commoners. Deer were so important not only because they were one of the largest game animals but also because, like humans, deer prefer corn. Maya mythology includes a story of the Sun God who turns into a deer to transport the Moon Goddess away from danger (Figure 2.3). Deer haunches were a particularly important offering in Maya rituals, and there may have been some sort of equivalency between the two sacred corn-eaters, deer and humans.

After attending to small animals, household members would also check on the many plants that filled domestic patios. Maya cities have been described as "garden cities" because there was so much space between structures and household groups. Soil chemistry indicates these open areas were used for planting nutrient-rich fruits, vegetables, and spices. Open patio spaces between the three to four structures in a residential compound were busy working areas shaded by fruit trees surrounding raised-bed and container gardens where herbs were grown. By building a small pen and raising it off the ground, Maya gardeners could protect their most delicate herbs from tropical pests including the domesticated ducks or turkeys who loved to nibble young shoots. As with the raised bed, repurposing a cracked water jar or other container as a planter allowed Maya gardeners to enhance the soil with natural fertilizers such as wood ash or other organic debris. This made raised-bed and container gardens very productive and sustainable. Peppers of various kinds that provided high amounts of vitamin C as well as spiciness and other culinary herbs like epazote were grown in these beds.

Avocado, guava, sapodilla, black and white zapote, and guava trees provided delicious fruit nearly year-round. All these plants are native to the Maya area and have now become famous around the world. Some were planted in natural solution holes in the bedrock that held moisture; others were planted in the ground surrounding structures.

FIGURE 2.3 Classic period ceramic vase of supernatural deer in conversation with an Old God of the underworld. University of Miami Special Collections, Jay I. Kislak Collection. 1987.014.00.0003. Photo by Justin Kerr, K4012, Dumbarton Oaks, Trustees for Harvard University, Washington. University of Miami Special Collections, Jay I. Kislak Collection.

Interspersed with the trees were other fruits like papaya, passionfruit, and dragon fruit. Maya people also grew beans, chili peppers, chaya or bush spinach, and achiote or annatto – a bright orange seed used as a seasoning for their complex cuisine. Likewise in the domestic garden there were medicinal plants like trumpet tree, whose leaves were used in a tea to treat digestive troubles, and ceremonial plants like balche, a tree whose bark was used to make a mildly alcoholic mead. Flowers were important in Maya art and rituals, and household compounds may have had plumeria or frangipani trees with its five-petaled white, pink, or yellow flowers, and an amapola tree whose dramatic pink bottlebrush flowers attract birds and bees.

Since Maya people did not have animals that provided wool, gardens also had plants useful for creating thread and cloth such as cotton, ceiba, and various agaves. Wild cotton was domesticated in Mexico, and it grew in a variety of colors from white to beige to brown that were easily dyed in a variety of colors. The ceiba tree, which can grow up to 200 feet tall, was a powerful symbol to ancient Maya people of the interconnectedness of the earth, the sky and the underworld

The Domestic World

FIGURE 2.3 (*cont.*)

(Figure 2.4). It also created seed pods filled with soft fibers that could be used as insulation or for filling cushions and sleeping mats and were even spun into thread. Agaves are succulents that thrive in the dry soils of the Maya world and have many useful components. By removing the flesh from agave leaves, Maya people exposed strong fibers that could be made into rope or twine, and even woven into burlap-style cloth.

While the garden was tended and ripe fruits harvested, a female head of the family likely began preparing the daily meal. In addition to corn pozole in the morning, people who left the compound for their daily tasks, such as men and young boys who had to walk to the cornfields, would take a ball of corn masa with them and perhaps some leftover tamales. People who stayed in the compound all day, like the children, elderly, and most of the women, snacked on masa, fruit, and other leftovers all day long. Later in the afternoon the family would gather together for one larger meal, such as turkey tamales with beans that had been slowly steaming in a cooking pot all day or, if the family was not as fortunate, ground ramon nut and bean tamales. Chaya or bush spinach was added to the corn masa and increased the nutritional value dramatically. Tamales were served with a variety of salsas made from avocado, chili peppers, achiote, and other seasonings. Tamales and other stewed dishes were served in large lipped

FIGURE 2.4 *Ceiba speciosa*, the sacred tree of the ancient Maya. Selva Lacandona, Chiapas, Mexico. Photo: Martina Katz / imageBROKER / Getty Images.

plates that held the contents in their sauce. People had smaller ceramic or gourd bowls from which they ate their own portions. Most of the population likely never had the opportunity to drink the hot, frothy chocolate that queens and kings consumed on special occasions, but they had plenty of fruit to mix with water for a nutritious and delicious beverage.

Early in the day family members would attend the ancestral shrine located on the eastern edge of the residential compound. These small platforms held the remains of beloved family members along with a few small offerings such as their favorite bowl or ornament. In one compound the funeral of a dear grandmother known as Sak Kab', or White Earth, took place only a week ago, and the plaster covering the cavity where she was buried in the ancestral platform was still soft. The funeral had to take place quickly after she died – within a day or two. Her body was wrapped tightly in cloth in the flexed position – with knees to chin – and soft powdery limestone, the whitest that could be found, was placed into the platform cavity to prepare the space. As prayers were said the bundle of her body was interred into the spot where so many other family members had been buried before her, including the founder of this family's line, who was the original settler that built the household compound occupied now for generations. A tiny amount of precious powdered red hematite obtained from a trader was sprinkled over the cloth wrapped body of Sak Kab', and finally her eating bowl and a small bead made of limestone were placed over her head to protect her soul from any dangers as she crossed into the underworld. The bead was painted a light bluish green that made it resemble the precious jade beads worn by the queen, a stately women seen at a distance once by Sak Kab' many years ago. Now the family would visit the ancestral shrine and talk to her spirit every day, telling stories about how her grandchildren were thriving and how her favorite ceiba tree was about to flower. In this way, all the ancestors of the extended family remained close members of the compound, involved in the day-to-day life of their descendants. On the tenth anniversary of her death they would reopen the cavity on the platform and offer her a new ceramic bowl or something else she would have liked, but this was a long while off and they had plenty of time to plan what to give her (Figure 2.5).

Simple burials are found in modest domestic structures throughout the Maya area in the Classic period, and they are our best evidence that ancestor veneration was practiced at all social levels, not just among the elite. However, even though such burials are common, there are not enough of them to account for the entire urban population. And yet there were no cemeteries in ancient Maya settlements. From these facts we conclude that certain individuals, maybe the family member who first established the domestic compound, or someone who accumulated prestige for their skill or influence, were chosen to be the revered ancestor, while other family members were not. Many commoner individuals are unaccounted for in death – perhaps they were cremated, perhaps they were buried in a manner that has yet to be discovered by archaeologists. But ancestor

FIGURE 2.5 Domestic burial of an ancestor with ceramic vessels and shell offerings in structure 9M-136, from the site of Xuenkal, Mexico. Photograph by the author.

veneration of certain individuals was an important part of domestic ritual life, and by analogy to other cultures, these beloved dead continued to exert influence in the lives of family members for many generations.[1]

CRAFT ACTIVITIES

Many productive activities took place in the household compound. Ancient Maya cities, no matter how large, did not have large-scale

[1] McAnany 2013.

workshops or warehouses as did the ancient cultures of Peru or Egypt; instead, almost every tool, object, piece of clothing, or work of art was made in a domestic setting by related family members. Archaeologists call this segmented production, and it is the best explanation of the particular archaeological materials related to crafting that are recovered from Maya households. Often objects found by archaeologists in domestic settings were unfinished, or multiple nearly identical objects are found. Both of these patterns are examples of the kind of material evidence that domestic production leaves behind. Making objects such as ceramic vessels or obsidian knives were activities that people folded into their daily routine, balanced alongside other daily tasks such as cooking and childcare or done after time spent away from the home in the fields and forests. Children or adults who moved into a compound learned how to craft tools and other necessities by observing expert craftspeople. Apprenticeship was informal and involved experimentation with materials and techniques under the supervision of a more experienced family member. In this sense the majority of ancient Maya people did not spend the entire workday engaged in a single activity as we do today; rather, they were expert multitaskers who produced goods needed by their household with extra goods paid to the state. Some members of Maya society who lived in palace compounds such as scribes or astronomers were obviously specialists and dedicated immense amounts of time to their art or craft (Figure 2.6). They did not have to spend time raising or preparing their own food, and their clothing and tools were provided by the goods made in commoner homes and paid in tribute to the elite. Overall, the ancient economy was based on surplus production in a household setting, a space filled with people of different skill levels and abilities who likely pooled their time and energy to complete many of the productive activities that occupied their days.

Without a large number of domesticated animals to provide wool or fur, almost all clothing was made of plant fibers in ancient Maya society. Plant fibers are versatile and abundant, but require a great deal of processing. Cotton must be cleaned of seeds, combed, and then spun into thread. Agave and henequen fibers must be cleaned of pulp and dried before they can be twisted into rope. In ancient painted bark-paper books and almanacs that survive today, known as codices, Maya women are depicted doing these activities in their household gardens.

FIGURE 2.6 Elaborate "eccentric" flint ornament made by a master craftsperson. The imagery shows three lords in profile. Courtesy of the Lowe Art Museum, 85.0078.

Four codices survive today from the Classic period, after many hundred were destroyed by Spanish clerics in a misguided effort to convert Maya people to Christianity. Ceramic and wooden spindle whorls attached to a wooden shaft were spun within a small gourd to draw the plant fibers down into a thin line of thread as fibers were spun together. Women sat together outside in the shade of their gardens spinning thread and weaving cloth. Young girls learned to spin by the time they were seven or eight years old, and older women whose children were grown and no longer had as much responsibility to manage a household also spent their time spinning.

This thread was later used to create elaborate cloth on the backstrap loom, a simple but powerful piece of technology still in use in the Maya area today. Backstrap looms allow the weaver to make a single length of cloth as wide as their hips but many meters long. The weaver can then stitch together multiple lengths of cloth to create nearly any piece of clothing, such as loincloths, headdresses, dresses, or blankets. One of the technological advantages of the backstrap loom is the ability of the weaver to see every aspect of the cloth as it is made and to adjust the tension of the cloth by leaning in or away from their work. This facilitated elaborate brocade work, a form of decoration where additional thread is added by the weaver into the warp and weft of the cloth. Patterns familiar in Maya art were often added to ancient cloth, such as animals like jaguars or birds, or the kan-cross (an equal armed cross that symbolized the world tree). Most Maya people wore simple clothing made of henequen or agave fibers, which would feel scratchy to us but were made of sturdy materials that were easy to obtain. On special occasions they may have worn clothing made of soft cotton, or leather, decorated with bird feathers or rabbit fur. In Maya art we see people wearing leather sandals or walking barefoot. Jewelry was also an important part of everyone's costume. Common folk wore shell or stone pendants, or a carved bone hairpin. From the ceramic figurines often found in domestic compounds, a variety of head gear including wide brimmed hats and elaborate hairstyles were also very common, as were tattoos and scarification in delicate spirals and swirls. Cloth was needed for many things in addition to clothing: food was gathered in cloth bundles, people carried goods to market in cloth, and in the urban palaces people slept behind cotton curtains on soft cotton mats. Thick bundles of cotton cloth were given as tribute payments to queens and kings by their subjects and by visitors from nearby polities.

Other plant fibers were just as important to the ancient Maya economy even if they were not used for clothing. Palm fibers harvested from the forest were used to weave baskets, mats, and hats and to make all manner of ropes and cordage. Palm fibers are pliable when they are first harvested and have to be used quickly before they dry out and become brittle. In addition to gourds, palm fiber baskets were likely the most common form of container in the ancient Maya economy. Durable and lightweight, a person who wanted to bring in corn from their milpa or to transport raw chert or obsidian from the mountains, or who had captured wild birds for their decorative feathers likely used a palm fiber net or basket to transport such commodities. Entire palm fronds lashed with agave fiber rope were used to roof the majority of structures in Maya cities, and, while waterproof, these roofs were under constant repair. The domestic houses of the Maya, with their plaster floors and thatched roofs, stayed cool in the tropical heat – air passed through a thatched roof, and the high pitch helped hot air move up and away from the living area. Plaster or tamped earth floors also stayed cool in the dark shade the thatch provided.

Another important activity that took place in the domestic compound was the manufacture of pottery and all forms of ceramic technology.

Ancient Maya people did not work metal until the last few centuries before European contact, when it was used for decorative purposes. They had an abundance of other container materials available from the plant and mineral worlds, including a wide variety of clays and powdered temper, which are the inert materials added to clay to enhance its elasticity and ability to withstand firing. They began experimenting with fire-hardening, or firing, clay in the Middle Formative period (as early as 800 BCE), and by the Classic period (200–800 CE) when Coba was occupied, potters excelled at using clay to create a huge assortment of different containers and objects of art. In the domestic setting, clay from the forest was stored under palm fronds to keep it damp. When time allowed an entire family would join together to process the raw clay into a usable material – children and older people could pick out plants or rocks in the clay, adults could knead additives or temper into the clay to make it stronger and more pliable. Children learned to make clay vessels when given small amount of clay to play with, and their miniature practice vessels are found in domestic excavations.[2] As the individuals who spent the most time in domestic compounds, women and girls likely made many of the ceramics used by their families. Large water jars, plates for serving food, and small bowls for drinking corn pozole were all simple forms that could be made in the garden while simultaneously supervising children and domestic animals. The potter's wheel was not utilized in this area of the world prior to European contact, and instead each piece was unique, made of slabs and coils, worked with a pebble until it was perfectly smooth (Figure 2.7).

Once ceramic vessels were formed they were left to dry in the sun, perhaps in a part of the garden area off-limits to small children and animals. When dry to the touch they were painted with a thin clay slurry or slip, and the colors of these slips changed slowly over time as ceramic technology improved. In addition to slip, ceramics were decorated with beeswax that burned off during firing, leaving a resist design, often of spirals or swirls such as found on the flat interior of serving plates. Later the painted vessels would be piled up carefully on an exposed area of bedrock within the garden, and a hot burning fire made of palm fronds and other slower burning wood was set alight on top of the vessels. This

---

[2] Sheets 2006.

The Domestic World

FIGURE 2.7 Modern Tzeltal Maya potter in the highlands of Guatemala using a traditional methodology. Photo: Insights / Contributor / Universal Images Group / Getty Images.

part of the process, known as open firing, was the most delicate and required considerable skill, although once the fire was set, anyone in the family compound could have supervised the firing and added more fuel as needed. The next day when the fire had burned itself out and the vessels were cool to the touch, family members could see which water jars or bowls had survived and which had cracked in the firing process. A cracked jar or plate might not be usable to serve food but it could be broken into pieces and those sherds could be repurposed as spindle whorls or fishing net weights. In some place broken sherds from "wasters," the objects that did not fire correctly, were ground up to be used as temper in future ceramic production.

Ancient Maya people also made many beautiful figurines from clay. These ranged from very plain figures with no facial features or only simple indentations to extremely elaborate costumed representations of royalty and mythological figures. The most intricate figurines were likely produced in the city center within artistic compounds where craftspeople had access to the details of costume and headdress necessary to accurately portray a ballplayer or court dancer. But the majority of figurines were unpretentious and made in domestic compounds alongside the manufacture of ceramic containers. These anthropomorphic representations were sometimes made in molds, so they could be produced rapidly and with a standardized set of imagery, but just as often they were made individually by hand. By adding two or more perforations to the body, it was easy to transform the hollow body of the figurine into an ocarina or simple flute. Whistle figurines were often made in the form of songbirds, other animals, and clowns but female bodies were a very common theme for figurines in the Classic period. Sometimes dressed in elaborate embroidered huipiles, the Maya name for tunics, and sometimes undressed, these figurines are identifiable as female by their clothing and elaborate hairstyles. Often, they carry children and wear broad-brimmed hats that suggest a person headed out into the sun to trade wares in the market or to fetch water.

Headdresses, hairstyles, and hats were all ways the head was adorned and marked in Maya art, which used the face and head as a potent canvas for social identity expression. Hairstyles changed when a woman married; nobles wore elaborate headdresses made of paper, jade, and shell and spent hours getting facial tattoos. Figurines in a wide variety of forms were a ubiquitous part of Classic period domestic life and perhaps played a role in storytelling or rituals that centered on the intersection of official state mythologies and family life.

THE EVENING AND LEISURE

As the afternoon sun started to fade, members of the family would gather again in the patio area between houses. Children had been in the courtyard all day, playing with sticks and chasing ducklings. Their older siblings spent much of the day in the courtyard as well, tending to chores and learning how to craft the tools their family needed. Adults were busy cooking or tending to the cornfields; perhaps someone had made a trip into the forest to look for a special medicinal plant or traveled down the broad paved road into the city center to visit the market where goods from other lands were exchanged. Before dusk they gathered together for a final meal of the day as the tamales and beans were finally ready. Extra food was prepared for visitors, for after dark there was little light available to work on crafts or other chores and it was time for leisurely activities in the twilight. The evenings in this part of the city were dedicated to visiting with neighbors and family, playing games, and storytelling. Ancient Maya people did not make oil lamps or other similar tools to illuminate the evening, although they had beeswax available for candles. It is unlikely that modest households like the one we discuss here were able to keep much of the beeswax they generated, as it was highly prized by the noble families who lived in larger palatial compounds that were illuminated at night.

Within this part of the city, where simple homes with gardens and extended families were packed side by side, there might have been a family of people who had formerly been enslaved. The practice of slavery in Classic Maya times is not well understood, but 16th-century Spanish accounts of Postclassic Maya society make it clear that enslaved people lived, worked, and were traded in many Maya settlements of that era. Extrapolating from European views of Postclassic Maya life back to native institutions of the Classic period 500 years earlier is a challenging proposition – iconographic and hieroglyphic evidence from the Classic period depicts mostly elite captives and prisoners who may have been ransomed, as we will discuss later. There are few, if any, images of commoner slaves from this time. Yet from the better documented Aztec practices of slavery and the most trustworthy accounts of Maya life written by Spaniards, we can conclude that Classic Maya society was not likely to be a "slave society" but rather a society with people who were enslaved.[3] The former are cultures on which all economic and social relations are determined by the slave-master relationship. This was clearly not the case in Classic Maya culture. However, royalty, elites, and even those middle-society members with wealth may have "owned" enslaved people along with their other privileges of wealth, including more elaborate architecture and long-distance prestige goods such as jade or painted pottery.

---

[3] Restall 2009:13.

Archaeologists have so far failed to identify the households or burials of enslaved people from the Classic period, in part because their lives may not have differed dramatically from those of most commoners, who regularly experienced nutritional deprivation, physical violence, and debilitating work requirements. We do not think there was a permanent enslaved class, or that children were born into slavery – in Spanish descriptions of both Aztec and Maya slavery it is usually the result of misfortune or criminal activity. Maya people who stole food or goods might have become enslaved to those from whom they stole, a status that could be temporary and terminated with successful repayment.[4] But there is documentary evidence that some enslaved people were obtained through interpolity raids or as the result of being taken captive in war. These may have been primarily higher-status individuals, who were subject to ongoing humiliation for political purposes, or they may have been unfortunate commoners. An important characteristic of Classic Maya society is that it does not seem to have a social identity associated with slavery, and people did not spend their entire lives born into and subject to the type of ownership and institutional violence associated with slavery in the colonial New World. Individual ancient Maya people became enslaved during the course of their lives, and often their fortunes changed to allow them freedom before death. When someone worked off their debt or escaped from slavery, they must have sought out refuge with their extended family perhaps in neighborhoods like the one described here, where each family group provided for themselves far from daily interactions with the powerful Maya who might seek to recapture or further exploit a less fortunate person. Formerly enslaved people would have had much in common with our family, and evening visits from a woman who had stolen to feed her family or a man taken captive in war might have been routine.

One visitor that was due to stop by the residential group was the midwife Pichi', or guava in English, since a baby was born only a month before to one of the younger mothers who lived in the compound. Midwives were highly respected specialists who attended all the births in the neighborhood, and expert midwives were even called

---

[4] Restall et al. 2023.

to the palace when the queen and her court gave birth. The baby boy born a month ago was healthy, and all the family rituals after his birth had gone as planned. His mother went through a period of seclusion afterward and then visited the sweatbaths for physical and spiritual cleansing. Sweatbaths were located throughout the city. Some were built of stone and set into the ground; others were more perishable and made of wood with branches above ground. Special prayers were said inside the sweatbath when someone needed cleansing, and by spending time inside this metaphorical cave new mothers emerged feeling stronger and cleaner. All the adults knew how to perform a sweatbath and no one needed a priest or priestess for this particular ceremony. Women would go with their female relatives and men would go with their male friends.

When Pichi' arrived at the house, she checked the mother to make sure she was feeling well and then she checked the baby. He had received a name shortly after the seclusion period but it would change at seven or eight years of age when he learned the male activities that his father and uncles would teach him. She checked his cradle board, the two wooden planks that held his head flat and shaped the pliable frontal and occipital bones so he would have a handsome profile like all his male relatives.[5] Everyone in this family had their head shaped in the first year of life – older midwives and the grandmothers knew how to place the infant on the cradle board and how much pressure to apply to shape the bones of the skull without hurting the child. Anyone in the city who did not have a shaped head was considered to have been poorly cared for as a child, except those people whose wahy, or animal companion spirit, prohibited them from using the cradleboard – there were a few people like that, even in the palace. Pichi' massaged the mother's pelvic area to make sure her reproductive organs were back in the correct place and then massaged the baby with an oil that contained ground annatto seed so his skin would be reddish and healthy. After all this work she sat down to share a tamale and hear what news there was of the neighborhood.

After Pichi' left, there was time for games and stories. The moon was bright enough to play patolli, a game of chance played with beans

---

[5] Tiesler 2011.

instead of dice. A geometrical board was scratched into the dirt in the garden and two players would take turns moving their colored beans around the squares of the board. Some families had a woven mat with a board painted on it, and in the palace boards were permanently painted or inscribed into the stucco of a sleeping bench. Everyone in the city was crazy for the game, and some people even bet turkeys or fruit that they would win. Our family does not have enough extra food to allow betting but they loved to throw the marked beans and beat one another in the count of patolli squares.

While the patolli game was going on, grandfathers told stories about the constellations in the night sky. With little artificial light, at night nearly everyone in their neighborhood had an excellent view of the Milky Way, known as the White Road in Maya, and all the major constellations. Ancient Maya people wrote that their kings and queens passed into the underworld via the Milky Way when they died and "entered the white road." The end of the dry season and the approach of the rainy times could be predicted by the appearance and disappearance of certain major constellations like the three stars of the Great Turtle, which we call the belt of Orion today.[6] When this constellation was no longer visible in the night sky, the rains would soon arrive. Stories were told about other constellations that the Maya saw as a rattlesnake, scorpion, bird, and frog, among others. Everyone could pick out the bright planet Venus above the horizon when it appeared as an evening "star" and when it later reappeared as a morning "star."

As the moonlight faded, most of the family moved into their homes to roll out their sleeping mats. The day would begin again before dawn. For comfort and companionship family members slept next to one another, with the baby close to his mother so he could nurse through the night, and the younger boys together so they could whisper to one another while the rest of the family slumbered. The embers of the cooking fire just outside the door of the hut were banked before bed, so they would be easy to kindle in the morning. Dried corn had been put into water and lime to soak in preparation for tomorrow's corn dough. All the animals were in their pens and fed.

---

[6] Bricker and Bricker 2011.

The domestic world was at the heart of ancient Maya culture. Most ancient people spent a huge part of their lives in and around the domestic compound where they were born and where their female relatives had been born for many generations. These compounds were used for centuries, with slight modifications such as a new plaster floor or a patio enlargement. Even death did not separate most people from their homes, as ancestors were buried in nearby household shrines that were actively used for small-scale, personal rituals. The interior and exterior areas of residential compounds were the most familiar spaces of ancient lives, just as our homes are the most familiar parts of our lives today. But unlike our society, ancient Maya people spent many hours at home engaged in the manufacture of goods that were then traded and exchanged throughout their neighborhood, their city, and the region in which they lived. Households were largely self-sufficient and each of the members had important responsibilities no matter how young or how old. Many central aspects of Maya culture were generated in the practices that took place inside the private family area of the residential compound. These intimate family practices were carried out at every home throughout the city, and much of what it meant to be a Maya person was knowing that other modest families also told stories about the stars, also played patolli, and also made pottery. These shared daily practices and the expectation of their perpetuation made life in the city meaningful.

Suggested Readings

Bricker, Harvey M., and Victoria R. Bricker 2011 *Astronomy in the Maya Codices*. Philadelphia: American Philosophical Society.

Callaghan, Michael 2016 Observations on Invisible Producers: Engendering Pre-Columbian Maya Ceramic Production. In *Gendered Labor in Specialized Economies*, ed. S. Kelly and T. Ardren, pp. 267–300. Boulder: University Press of Colorado.

Halperin, Christina 2014 *Maya Figurines: Intersections between State and Household*. Austin: University of Texas Press:.

Hutson, Scott R. 2010 *Dwelling, Identity, and the Maya: Relational Archaeology at Chunchucmil*. Walnut Creek, CA: AltaMira Press.

Sheets, Payson 2006 *The Ceren Site: An Ancient Village Buried by Volcanic Ash in Central America*. Belmont, CA: Thompson Wadsworth.

Tiesler, Vera 2011 Becoming Maya: Infancy and Upbringing through the Lens of Pre-Hispanic Head Shaping. *Childhood in the Past* 4:117–132.

3

Fields and Forest

Maize, or what most people in the United States call corn, was at the heart of ancient Maya culture. It provided the main source of calories, it was the main ritual offering and feast food, and corn deities were central to the guiding mythologies that made royal rulership possible. By the Classic period maize agriculture required constant attention as the plant had become completely dependent on human intervention through the domestication process. Maize is often depicted in Classic art as a delicate, young child, in need of protection. The shared practices of planting, tending, harvesting, and processing maize unified Maya communities and provided a keystone to their cultural identity. Indigenous growing techniques were refined for the tropical climate of the Maya area, but corn was still dependent on the arrival of regular rains, not always a guaranteed phenomenon in the tropics. Maya farmers were greatly assisted in securing agricultural success by the large beehives they kept at the edges of their fields. Native stingless bees produced honey and wax but were perhaps most important for their role in pollination of agricultural plants. Many wild resources were harvested from the rich rainforests that surrounded every settlement. The forests were places of unruly spirits and untapped potential. They were respected as reservoirs of plants, animals, and minerals needed for daily life. Research has shown that many of the forest management techniques used during the Classic period survive today in the most remote areas of the Maya world, and we have learned much about ancient plant and animal management from the modern

Fields and Forest 47

Indigenous people of southern Mexico, Belize, and Guatemala. Within the animate Maya landscape, filled with spirits of place, caves and underground sources of fresh water took on special significance. They were places to connect with the forces of creation and a primary location for rituals of fertility and rain.

PEOPLE OF MAIZE (AND OTHER FOODS TOO)

A day working in the maize field, or milpa, began early, likely just after dawn. Mostly fathers and younger men of the family left the household compound with a ball of corn dough wrapped in a simple cloth or large leaf and a gourd of drinking water. Later in the morning during a break in their work, they would mix some of this dough with water to make a porridge-like pick-me-up to fill their bellies. There were times when women of the household attended to the needs of the field as well – likely during harvest or when there were not enough male relatives in a family. Individual women might have preferred this type of work to the daily routine of the domestic compound. But our best research indicates that ancient Maya people understood the maize field as the domain generally of men, an area where they naturally excelled due not just to generally greater physiological strength but to the agreements made within Maya culture about the complementarity of daily tasks. Both the creation of raw foodstuffs by men and the transformation of those foodstuffs into cuisine by women were essential to daily life, and neither was more or less important in Maya society.

The complementarity of tasks required to render maize a useful food is signaled to us in the way ancient Maya people chose to represent the Maize Deity, or Juun Ixim (One Maize). It is likely the power of maize was not subsumed into a single deity, since the mother of the Hero Twins was considered a maize mother who could fill endless woven bags with corn by calling on her guardians of the field. But Juun Ixim is the more common depiction in Classic art (Figure 3.1). Youthful and beautiful, Juun Ixim is neither completely masculine nor completely feminine, but combines costume and physical elements usually associated with each gender in Maya art. Often bare above the waist, as royal men are commonly depicted, the Maize Deity has a very particular hairstyle, with one lock falling over the

FIGURE 3.1 Juun Ixim, the Maize Deity, from a carved vase found in a burial at Xuenkal, Mexico. Illustration courtesy of the Proyecto Arqueologico Xuenkal.

forehead, much like the tassels of a young ear of corn. Elaborately coiffed hair is more typical of the female gender in Maya art, where it signals the reproductive status and age of a woman. The gender fluidity of the Maize Deity is further indicated by their jade net skirt. Skirts are a costume element very clearly marked as female in Maya art, and are distinct from loincloths worn by men. The Maize Deity is often depicted in a jade net skirt, which can also include a large spondylus (spiny oyster) shell over the pelvic area, a clear reference to the creative power of the sea. Royal Maya women are shown wearing this bivalve shell girdle on stelae, and commoner women wore shell pendants over their pelvic area prior to marriage. Finally, Juun Ixim is often portrayed gracefully dancing, to convey an active sexuality that is usually the province of a group of young female deities. Thus many aspects of the Maize Deity, from costume to appearance to mythology, emphasize the dual gender or gender-fluid nature of the corn plant – and its importance as a representation of the most potent creative forces in the Mesoamerican universe.

As men and boys left their homes with bags of seeds, they also carried long, sharpened sticks to plant maize (and other seeds) and a slingshot to hunt for birds. They walked for an hour before reaching the cornfield that an extended family farmed together. During this walk they passed scores of other simple households like their own, each with families busy waking up and preparing to tend to their fields as well. Along the way they also passed a larger house, set upon a

Fields and Forest

plaster-covered platform, where the local lord lived. He was not royalty, like the people who lived in the center of the city, but he and his family made sure everyone who lived in simple houses paid their fair share of maize so the royal family and all their retinue did not have to spend time under the hot sun planting and tending maize. The exact mechanisms by which tribute, or in-kind wealth given to a higher-ranking member of society as a sign of allegiance, were extracted or delivered between farmers and elites is an area of active research within Maya studies at this moment.[1] Given the large size of Maya cities and the small number of royals, mid-level elites like this lord were likely crucial actors in the enforcement and documentation of tribute payments. His house was larger than those of most people, with walls made of carved stone rather than wood. But his roof was also thatched with palm fronds, like the majority of houses in this city, and he likely ate the same meals of corn tamales or pozole, with fruit and small amounts of meat, as any farmer might.

The cave with sacred water was not far from this lord's home. The family we are following in this book remembered traveling to the cave at different times, sometimes separated into groups of only women or only men; at other special occasions everyone could travel the paths that led to a stone stairway marked with carved faces. The faces watched as visitors descended from the surface down to the pools of cool, fresh water that could only be found inside a cave like this.[2] The walls of the cave sparkled in torchlight and it was easy to see the way to the offering spot. Important visitors had left their handprints in red on certain walls of the cave surrounding sacred pools. The faces showed the way to a large, open chamber where ceramic vessels with food and other offerings to the rain deities were left. Some of the stalactites and stalagmites had grown together and looked like a sacred tree; one of these underground trees was in the center of the chamber where freshwater pools were located. The rain deities loved this spot because this is where fresh rain water resided until Chac called it up into the sky to fall from storm clouds on the fields and forest. Caves were so filled with life force, so cool and dark and humid,

---

[1] Masson et al. 2020.
[2] Rissolo 2020.

that no one forgot the experience of traveling through them and back up to the hot, sunny ground at the edge of the village.

Gradually the houses grew further and further apart. Some of them were even set alone in a field, without a compound and patio for family members. Perhaps they were temporary shelters where someone lived until they could build something larger and friendlier with room for a growing family. A few looked like huts that were only used to take a shady nap during the middle of a long day spent in the maize field. Eventually, our family reached their cornfield and found it as they hoped – the bushy plants they had burned off a week ago were now cinders, although in some places small fires still smoldered. The fire had burned at a low enough temperature that some of the wood was carbonized rather than completely turned to ash, preserving many nutrients to enrich the soil. The younger men would scatter those fires and turn the ash under the topsoil. All that was left of the secondary growth forest they had burned were the trunks of the largest trees – they would plant their maize in neat rows around these reservoirs of soil nutrients.

For ancient Maya people the maize field was a cosmological model or map of the world. The field was square, with piles of stone at each of the corners to protect the plants from forest spirits and to mark out the four sacred directions. The maize and other plants were at the center of those four directions, just as Maya people lived at the center of the four cardinal directions. In native Maya books created prior to Spanish arrival, there are important ceremonies known as the Yearbearer rituals (Figure 3.2). Village leaders and ritual specialists walked from temples at the center of a settlement to stone markers at the edge of town, in each of the four cardinal directions.[3] These ceremonies took place in the last five days of the old year and involved an elaborate procession by priests and priestesses along a ritual circuit. Participants carried images of gods and various offerings to stone markers at the entrances to their town and then to the houses of respected villagers and finally to a temple in the center of the settlement. Statements in these books make clear that these processions were a ritualized reenactment of the events of creation. A key

---

[3] Vail and Hernandez 2013.

Fields and Forest

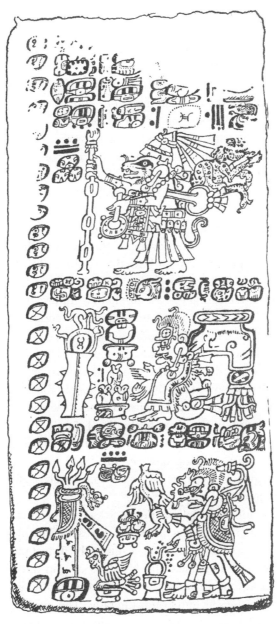

FIGURE 3.2 Yearbearer ceremonies on page 26 of the 1880 Forstemann facsimile of the Dresden Codex showing offerings from the cardinal directions. Photo by Gabrielle Vail.

component of the ceremony was marking out the space that defined the world of the living. Many, many aspects of Classic Maya life were arranged in a quadripartite system, or with a clear awareness of the four directions and the central point where four corners intersect. Setting up a maize field was another way to demonstrate and reinforce the importance of the cardinal directions and an ordered universe.

Maya houses were built on this same design, with the four corner posts acting as the trees at the edges of a cornfield framing an open living space in the center. The field was cleared from the surrounding forest, likely from forest that had been burned in the past but let rest fallow for at least ten years to rejuvenate. Old growth tropical forest, filled with precious medicinal plants, huge trees, and powerful animals, was protected as a resource bank and never burned for agriculture.[4] But along the border of the city and the forest was a wide band of land, with scrubby bush that could easily be burned back to create natural fertilizer for the thin acidic soils in this part of the world. The act of clearing out a maize field from the forest was potent for ancient Maya people, as it is for many Maya people today. It is an act of construction, making something good and right and productive from the wild and raw resources of the natural world. For this reason Maya people created their milpas the same way in the past as they do today, and all residents of the city created them in the same manner as their neighbors. Today Yucatec Maya farmers use the width of their hand, from the tip of the pinky to the tip of the thumb, and measure out ten hands' length. Twenty of those units make up a k'aan, and twenty k'aan units make up one side of a field (about a kilometer). Using this regularized system each extended family is allotted similar amounts of land.

Before beginning to plant, the men asked for permission from their deities, including the guardians of the earth. The prayer acknowledged the reciprocal nature of agriculture: by disturbing the surface of the earth, and asking for the blessings of rain and fertility, the farmer entered into a contract with the earth guardians to tend his crops, preserve the soil, and honor the rains. The local lord who lived in the raised platform stone house was said to have spoken to a priest

---

[4] Ford and Nigh 2015.

who could read the codices, the ritual almanacs that predicted planting times. For these farmers, the advice of a hieroglyphic codex was not necessary, as they had grown up learning how to predict the arrival of daily rains, but they were pleased to hear the almanac predicted that no pests would attack and eat their young maize shoots this year. The ritual cycle of agricultural planting and harvesting created a rhythm for Maya lives. In their youth, men learned how to watch for the signs that would suggest it was time to burn their fields in preparation for planting, and then they watched for when the rains would come. Most parts of the ancient Maya world did not have systems of irrigation, as in the ancient states of Egypt or the Andes, and so it was essential to plant only shortly before the daily summer rains began in order not to waste the seeds, which could shrivel and burn in the heat of the summer. Some families even waited until after the rains had started in earnest, although they were considered lazy since knowing when the rains were about to arrive was considered a common skill all men should possess.

Men carried a bag woven by their family members of sisal or agave fiber, which held three types of seeds. Using a long, sharpened stick to open a small hole in the earth, maize, beans, and squash seeds were all planted simultaneously in set quantities to make sure they grew strong together. After the farmer dropped the seeds into the cavity made with his planting stick, he stepped onto the hole to seal the seeds inside. With a normal pace he would repeat the same process over and over again, and in this manner a family of three or four men could plant their field in a few days. Every maize seed that grew into a stalk would provide a trellis for the beans to climb (Figure 3.3). And every fast growing squash provided ground cover to shade the tender young sprouts of corn. Together these three plants supported each other's growth cycle and increased their likelihood of growing to maturity. Furthermore, the nutrients that corn extracts from the soil, such as nitrogen, are replaced by the beans. This meant that in contrast to modern mono-cropping, where only corn is grown and the topsoil is exhausted of nutrients within a few years, ancient Maya people discovered how to prevent nutrient loss and keep their soils productive. Early in the archaeological investigation of ancient Maya society, scholars discovered that the Maya had very few domesticated animals and certainly did not eat animal protein on a regular basis. Soon

FIGURE 3.3 The Three Sisters growing together in Yucatan, Mexico. Young maize leaves rise above squash and bean leaves lower on the ground. Photograph by the author.

thereafter it was discovered that a diet of corn and beans eaten in combination creates a complete protein, or one that contains all essential amino acids, mimicking protein-rich animal products. Eaten alone, corn provides huge amounts of calories through sugars and carbohydrates, but is not particularly nutritious. Because Maya people also ate significant amounts of legumes, their bodies were able to combine the amino acids from both vegetable foods to create a complete protein and live healthfully with minimal dietary contributions from animal products. Thus the basis for ancient Maya diets was this Indigenous discovery of how to maximize the nutritional value of two native plants common in the region. The squashes native to the Maya region also provided important nutrients, not only in the vitamin-rich flesh, but in fat-rich seeds. Squash seeds were dried, roasted, and ground into a tasty powder that could be added to almost any dish or made into a delicious sauce for tamales and vegetables. Domesticated in Mexico, corn, beans, and squash – what many native people call the Three Sisters – spread up into North America and provided sustainable, complete nutrition for most Indigenous populations prior to European contact.

While corn was ideologically, nutritionally, and culturally very important to the ancient Maya, we are learning that many other foods were grown in complex agricultural features that took advantage of local microenvironments. The sloping hills of the Maya highlands were filled with stone walls built to retain soil as it washed down a mountainside. Wetlands along the coast were often canalized or drained to create rich planting beds for maize but also for carbohydrate-dense root crops such as manioc and American taro.[5] There are serious methodological challenges to documenting all the ways ancient Maya people utilized the environment to grow food, and in the past we relied too much on modern ethnographic accounts of slash and burn maize cultivation. It is clear that Classic Maya farmers spent time in a variety of food-growing environments, not just tending a milpa. Terraces offered a context where hillside erosion was prevented and cooler temperatures could be achieved in deeper soils, often soils that were enhanced by their caretakers. Wetland raised planting areas provided well-watered and rich soils, as well as access to natural fertilizer from the organic materials cleaned out of drainage canals. This nutrient-rich organic matter likely included fish or mollusks that could have provided nutrition to Maya people as well as to their agricultural soils, as better documented in the raised wet fields of central Mexico.

Diversifying their crops beyond the Three Sisters not only provided better nutrition; it also provided some measure of security against pests and disease. Maya agriculture undoubtedly varied tremendously across time and space, but by the Classic period most parts of the Maya area were densely occupied and unclaimed land was rare. This meant that occupants of an ancient city like Coba, even rural occupants, had to maximize the productivity of the land they had. Household gardens helped supplement food grown in dry fields, wetland raised fields, and

---

[5] Dunning et al. 2018.

terraces, as did wild food foraged from forest lands. But environmental archaeologists argue that in the Classic period, population levels were so high, and unclaimed land so scarce, that Maya farmers practiced a very delicate balancing act that likely made them vulnerable to episodic droughts, hurricanes, and other ambient challenges. Yet despite these factors, Maya farmers thrived successfully in a tropical climate for hundreds of generations.[6]

APICULTURE

While the older men focused on planting seeds that would feed their families and the royalty who protected their city, one of the younger boys collected disk-shaped pieces of limestone that he found in the newly burned field. These natural formations could be shaped into plugs the family used to seal their beehives. Yax Tuun, or Blue-Green Stone in English, wandered from the milpa to the edge of the forest, and signaled to his family members with a whistle that he was heading to check on their bees. After a short walk into the cool shade of the forest he came upon the hives. He wasn't afraid of this part of the forest – he knew it well and knew the paths that would lead him back to the field, or to a nearby well. There was little chance of running into a jaguar or tapir here, so close to human activity and the sunny, cleared agricultural fields. This part of the forest was filled with large flowering trees that the family of Yax Tuun had tended for generations because they provided the nectar needed to support their native Maya stingless bees. The bees in turn helped pollinate the maize, beans, and squash the family ate later in the summer after harvest. The location of the hives was carefully chosen by an ancestor many generations ago because it was close to the fields for pollination, close to a well so the bees had plenty of water, and surrounded by flowering trees and bushes that fed the bees before the agricultural plants flowered. The grandfathers of Yax Tuun taught him that certain bushes grew quickly and produced many flowers; these plants were allowed to grow on the edges of the agricultural field, again in order to help the bees.

Apiculture, or the tending of bees in order to facilitate pollination and harvest honey and wax, was a central component of the ancient

---

[6] Beach et al. 2020.

Maya agricultural system. Maize required constant tending, and bees helped the family with this work by increasing the agricultural yield through targeted pollination. By forcing their bees to forage on maize fields, it is likely that the bees helped rural farmers embedded in the agricultural system support the large populations of the Classic period. Native Maya bees also produce honey, which was used for making the alcoholic drink balche. It was the only alcoholic beverage the ancient Maya consumed that we know of today, and it was a necessary component of every ceremonial occasion. Honey was used for medicinal purposes, to treat wounds, eye ailments, and to strengthen the immune system. Like many bee-keeping cultures, ancient Maya people also consumed royal jelly, pollen, and even bee larvae for their rich nutrients. (Pollen has more protein per ounce than steak!) Beeswax and pine resin torches may have been the primary source of artificial light in the evenings, and beeswax was used as a sealant, in wax-resist decorations of ceramic vessels and cloth, and as an important item to trade with people who lived on the coast where bees are difficult to raise.

Yucatan is filled with many species of native bees, and during the 16th century new Spanish overlords extracted vast quantities of honey and beeswax from the Maya people living in this region. Bishop Diego de Landa in his 16th-century recollection of life in Yucatan stated that "of honey this country is very abundant, and the honey is very good save for the fact that it comes out somewhat watery because the food of the bees is very fertile, so it is necessary to heat it over fire, and that makes it very good and very hard."[7] Ancient Maya people chose to befriend a small, gentle, and stingless bee known as *Melipona beecheii*, or xunan kab in Maya, which means "royal lady." In the wild these bees live in hollow tree logs, and Maya beekeepers replicated this habitat by cutting lengths of a certain naturally hollow tree and stacking these lengths one atop the other on an A-framed structure made of wood. Each frame could hold around twenty logs, and each log held a hive with its queen. Inside the logs the bees formed a unique type of comb that held their thin, clear honey (Figure 3.4). The hollow logs were plugged on both ends with limestone or wooden

---

[7] Restall et al. 2023.

FIGURE 3.4 Xunan Kab native Maya stingless bees kept in a hollow log in Yaxunah, Yucatan, Mexico. Photograph by the author.

disks, carved to fit tightly into the opening. A single hole was drilled into the side of each log so the bees could enter and exit the hive, and when it was time to harvest the honey or beeswax, a Maya beekeeper removed a stone plug and poured the honey into a container using a woven basket that strained out any debris. Once the bees had left the hive, the beekeeper could remove the wax, being careful to leave enough for the hive to rebuild. Bee-keeping was of such practical and ideological significance that the creator deity Itzamna is shown guarding beehives and offering balche in the Maya native book known as the Madrid Codex.[8] Tropical bees are active year round, and do not hibernate like European bees. Harvesting their honey and beeswax was tied to the annual rhythm of rains: when the rains first appeared

---

[8] Vail and Dedrick 2020.

Fields and Forest

in the spring and caused the flowers to bloom, the bees produced their maximum quantity of honey. In the fall when temperatures cooled and the rains had stopped, the bees rested and produced less. This Indigenous apiculture tradition lives on today in Yucatan, where some families have maintained their xunan kab hives for generations.

As the young Yax Tuun approached the beehives, he said a little prayer to the bee deity, a gentle spirit that understood the needs of humans to eat maize but who deserved great respect for the contribution of bees to so many things that were necessary to life in the ancient city. He picked up a few stones that had fallen out of the simple wall that surrounded the base of the beehive frame, so no raccoons or tayra weasels could rob the honey his family loved so much. He checked the western side of the wall where the ceramic figurine of the bee deity that his grandmother brought back long ago from a trip to the coast was still there in the small niche made to protect it. He touched the figurine gently and remembered all the stories he learned about how the Hero Twins were expert beekeepers, and why it was important for all Maya people to respect bees. Yax Tuun noticed that the simple thatched roof over the beehives needed repair and he set off down the path to look for the correct type of palm thatch. This was an easy chore and he enjoyed walking these paths through the shady forest and listening to birds. But it would also make his family happy that he had taken the time to ensure the bees were safe and well tended.

THE FOREST

On their way to and from tending maize fields, or sometimes as part of a special trip at night, ancient Maya men went into the forest to hunt wild game. Most of the birds and small animals eaten by ancient Maya people were found in the secondary forest that grew in abandoned agricultural fields, especially deer, the most highly prized wild food served on important ceremonial occasions. Secondary forest was generated when a milpa field was allowed to remain fallow for many years, a necessary step in maintaining soil fertility. Dangerous large mammals such as jaguars, peccary, monkeys, and tapir lived deeper in the old growth forest, far from human activity. It is possible that only the royalty were allowed to hunt jaguar, and there were strong taboos against eating it, as one never knew if the jaguar was a king or queen traveling about at night in their animal companion form. But wild turkeys, a bird similar to a pheasant known by the melodious name chacalaca (*Ortalis vetula*), wild pigs known as peccary, and deer were common in the bushy secondary forest where a milpa field had been left unsown. They foraged on the squash that continued to regrow for years after the fields were left fallow, and the insects that foraged, in turn, on the squash. The tangled bushy plants of an untilled field provided a safe refuge for small animals and game birds that were an easy way for hunters to attract larger game.

Isotopic analysis of ancient skeletons has shown that most inland Maya people, including the royalty, obtained about 75 percent of their calories from maize. As discussed earlier in this chapter, when eaten in combination, corn and beans provide a complete protein. There were very few domestic animals in ancient Maya cities: dogs were kept as hunting companions and in some cases for food,[9] ducks and turkeys were raised for food, and perhaps deer were raised for ritual purposes and as pets. Spanish accounts describe Maya people allowing deer to eat at the edges of cornfields and even being fed within household compounds, although zooarchaeological evidence for the full domestication of deer is equivocal. Wild game was a culturally important part of the diet, although the calories and protein provided by animals played a relatively small nutritional role in ancient lives.

The majority of ancient Maya people lived well inland from the coast, and the animals they ate reflect the landscape in which they traveled and lived. Animal bones are found preserved in middens, or trash heaps, near residential areas, in kitchens, behind palace structures, and even inside platforms when ancient people chose to utilize their trash as construction fill. Remains of white-tailed deer are the most common food debris found, by far, and at some sites deer bones make up over 50 percent of the faunal remains. In part this is due to the fact that deer bone is sturdy and holds up well in the acidic soils of the tropics. Peccary, also known as javelinas, are a New World native wild pig that was also an important part of the ancient Maya diet. Like most pigs, peccary are very intelligent and hunting them required

---

[9] Cunningham-Smith et al. 2020.

Fields and Forest 61

more skill and cunning than hunting deer. Tapir are an even larger pig-like mammal whose closest relative is actually the donkey. These shy, herbivorous mammals lived in the deep forest but were occasionally hunted for food. Other than these large animals, ancient Maya people ate small game such as rabbits, gophers, and armadillos, although apparently not opossum or raccoon. They hunted game birds and waterfowl but rarely ate reptiles such as turtles or iguanas, until later in the Classic period when other game may have been scarce. Fish and other marine resources were consumed primarily on the coast. Certain animals with high ceremonial significance such as large cats, monkeys, or parrots were never eaten regularly.

Men who planned to hunt carried with them a blowgun and small clay pellets.[10] The blowgun was made of a hollow wooden tube often longer than the person using it. A skilled hunter can be incredibly accurate with a blowgun, and even small game birds like quail could be killed with a single shot. After thirteen kills, a blowgun had to be ritually cleansed of the problems associated with taking so much life from the guardians of the earth. This historic ritual, which may have its origin in the pre-Columbian period, asks for the understanding of the deities of the forest and lets the hunter continue to search for food without the risk of injury.[11] If the ritual is not performed, a blowgun can break, the game will not appear in sight of the hunter, or his weapons can turn against him. Blowguns appear in ancient Maya art depicting the adventures of the Hero Twins, who used blowguns to hunt birds and defend themselves in the underworld. Hunting larger game from the old growth forest was done with woven nets to catch unsuspecting prey that were then dispatched with blades made of obsidian or chert (Figure 3.5). Ancient Maya books include images of large game such as deer or peccary caught with a foot-snaring noose hung over a tree branch by a patient and wily hunter. Young boys learned how to hunt small game such as rabbits and birds with a slingshot, and all men carried this weapon with them on their daily travels outside the domestic compound in case they had the good fortune to come across a gopher or the bad fortune to see a dangerous snake. Older men who liked hunting would often go out

---

[10] Ventura 2003.
[11] Anderson and Medina Tzuc 2005.

FIGURE 3.5 Hunter with blade-tipped spear on a Classic period ceramic vase. Photo: Lowe Art Museum, 2009.26.

alone to track and stalk a deer based on their knowledge of its habits. They might go out at sundown or sunrise to increase their chances and use calls to imitate the sound of a fawn and attract a mother deer. Sometimes an entire family of men with their hunting dogs would encircle an overgrown field to flush out whatever prey they could find and, with slingshots and blowguns, bring home as much meat as possible. One or two men would attempt to herd the deer and other animals toward the other hunters. The grandfather of our family owned a conch shell horn and liked to tell the story of how he could blow the conch to signal that it was time for the men to run into the bush and herd animals toward the hunters.

More serious hunting for a large tapir or fat peccary relied on careful techniques of patient tracking and calls. Using information available in the forest, ancient Maya hunters identified the movements of large game by their tracks and knowledge of their preferred habitats. Hunters also used tough but flexible leaves from forest trees to imitate the calls of many birds and small animals to lure them closer. It is likely that ancient Maya hunters kept specially trained dogs to help with hunting, as many Maya hunters do today. These dogs help identify the presence of game, flush game, and can even retrieve birds, rabbits, and paca, a large, fruit-eating, terrestrial rodent. Today, even modest families will lavish resources on an excellent game dog who accompanies his master on all his trips into the forest.

CAVES AND CAVE RITUAL

Just as farmers had to speak with the earth guardians before they planted, other important features of the landscape also held potency and spiritual power. Caves, wells, springs, and rock shelters were places where the underworld and the surface world met – passageways or portals where humans could access other spiritual realms. The entire landscape was animate in Maya belief; mountains, forests, maize fields, and caves were living sentient beings with agency and unique spiritual powers that could impact humans. But watery places like caves and springs were especially meaningful components of the landscape. Water is an essential ingredient to life, and the power of water was understood by ancient Maya people to be both beneficent and malevolent. Many parts of the Maya area lack perennial surface water, and almost all of the area experiences a five-month-long dry season during which there is limited precipitation. In the tropics the annual seasons are wet and dry. During the summer torrential rains arrive daily to nourish crops, but hurricanes can wipe out a village or cause flooding and crop failure. Some regions have no rivers at all, so natural sinkholes, or cenotes, provided the only natural source of drinking water for many large ancient cities. These features were augmented with wells that people dug and lined with cut stone or cisterns carved from the limestone bedrock that could hold rainwater.

While cenotes were an important economic resource and often the impetus for new settlements, some of the largest Classic Maya cities

FIGURE 3.6 Cave with collapsed roof. Small flags identify artifacts in the process of being recorded. Photograph by Donald A. Slater.

had no natural water sources and relied entirely on rainwater catchment systems and distribution. Maintaining a balance between too little water and too much was a constant preoccupation. The fair and equal management of drinking water was a key responsibility of leaders and may have been one of the primary drivers in the evolution of social complexity.[12] Systems of water sharing required enforcement, and rainwater collection features such as cisterns or collection pools demanded maintenance. Some scholars have suggested that early leaders who engineered these systems facilitated larger settlements and engendered the respect of their peers.

Many caves in the Maya area contain springs or pools of fresh water. The porous limestone geology of the region allows freshwater streams to run deep below the ground surface. Frequently, the soft limestone collapses and provides access to this water in the form of a cave or sinkhole. Around Coba a common form is the collapsed dome cave, in which the roof of a bedrock chamber gives way to allow access to the cavernous underground space below (Figure 3.6). Using a rope or

[12] Lucero 2006.

wooden ladder, ancient Maya people entered caves from the surface and explored the areas illuminated by narrow shafts of sunlight that burst through the opening. Evidence from cave excavations shows that sometimes torches made of pine wood covered in pitch were burned for light; ceremonies were conducted in the darker recesses where sunlight did not reach. They built stairways, platforms, and small pyramids inside these caves with limestone blocks shaped within the cave. Food offerings were left in cave rituals, and cave water may have been retrieved, as it is today because this water is considered especially powerful and sacred.

The fresh water found in caves, sometimes as a long meandering river and more commonly as a deep cenote connected to the underground aquifer, was a crucial component of many rituals. Maya people understood that the earth was the source of life-giving water; rain, lightning, and rainbows all originated in the earth and moved up into the sky. Souls that had died went into the watery underworld and those about to be born emerged from the same place. Caves were like wombs: steamy, wet chambers of generative force. These places were alive and their breath could be felt at every entrance, in a phenomenon we describe today as the result of differences in atmospheric pressure. Humans were understood to have originated in a sacred cave deep in a mountain. Queens and kings commissioned their final resting chambers, usually in the form of a tomb set deep inside a pyramidal temple, to replicate the original cave inside the primordial mountain. Many features of the built environment – tombs, pyramids, even sweatbaths – were human-designed echoes of the sacred natural landscape. Rituals to petition rain deities were performed in caves in order to entice the movement of their generative watery power up from the underworld and into the sky. All the men in our family had experienced cave rituals. Men and women often visited different caves at different times of their lives. Some caves were known by only the most holy priests who visited them on certain days of the year. Others were large enough to hold 200 people and the setting for familiar rituals dedicated to the rain guardians (Figure 3.7). A few years back, the men of our family had done rain-calling rituals over and over again as the hot, dry spring lingered on into summer. The first time they purified themselves and left offerings of maize stalks, bean pods, and whole squash for the underworld deities. When that was not

FIGURE 3.7 Balancanche Cave, Mexico. The central chamber of this cave, in which a stalactite and stalagmite have grown together in a form that resembles the sacred ceiba tree, is large enough to hold hundreds of people. Ceramic offerings to rain deities were left in antiquity. Photograph by Donald A. Slater.

sufficient to bring the rains needed for their crops, they returned with jars of fermented balche and fruit juice, hoping the liquid offerings would convince their deities of what was needed. They made a final trip, with all the young boys of the family and the oldest grandfathers, to spend an entire night praying under the illumination of hot pine torches. They burned copal incense and left fruit and forest offerings such as avocado and cohune palms on the platforms near the water pool.[13] Thankfully, this final massive offering by the community was successful and the rains arrived.

Sweatbaths were built in every large ancient Maya city to recreate the intoxicating and purifying powers of a steamy underground grotto. Known as pibna or oven house in the inscriptions of Palenque and other major cities, sweatbaths were architectural constructions with multiple meanings. They served utilitarian and medicinal purposes of cleansing the body but also a spiritual purpose. The

---

[13] Morehart et al. 2005.

two were not seen as distinct. Often subterranean and made of stone masonry, ancient Maya sweatbaths were small, holding maybe six people at a time. A "firebox" was usually contained within the walls and connected to the main chamber by a floor channel, through which hot air entered the sweatbath.[14] A small door helped contain the heat and often benches were built into the walls. A simpler wooden version was found preserved in the volcanic eruption that covered the site of Ceren, in El Salvador, and from this we believe modest sweatbaths were built in villages as well as in cities. Sweatbaths played an important role in women's lives, as settings for pre- and post-partum sweats, births, and perhaps rituals after first menstruation. The purification powers of the sweatbath were so important in ancient Maya culture that in hieroglyphic inscriptions royal structures were described metaphorically as sweatbaths of deities.[15]

As much as the domestic world was at the heart of Maya culture, the field and forest were at the heart of Maya spirituality. Classic Maya society was built on a sophisticated understanding of the natural world based on thousands of years of trial and error by early gardeners, farmers, and hunters. By careful observation of plant and animal behavior they perfected a complex system of natural resource management and utilization. Delicately balancing the needs of large populations against the resources of a tropical environment required expert knowledge of the natural world and how it could be harnessed to human civilization in a sustainable manner. Maize agriculture, when practiced using Indigenous traditions of companion planting (sowing different plants in proximity to increase crop productivity, pest control, or pollination) in soils enhanced through nutrient maximization, and perhaps coupled with calorie-rich root crops that are difficult to detect in the archaeological record, provided the nutritional resources necessary for dense urban populations in thousands of cities across the lowlands. Farming techniques, learned within the family but replicated across the entire Maya region, were a fundamental means by which Maya people practiced what it meant to be Maya, and demonstrated their shared identity to one another. Water management was practiced in different ways depending on available

[14] Hammond and Bauer 2001.
[15] Houston 1996.

natural resources, but it was an aspect of life that kept Maya people cooperating and competing with one another. Conscientiously managed forest resources provided not only a nutritional supplement to agriculture, but medicinal and spiritual assets as well. Native stingless bees were perhaps the greatest friend to Maya agriculture, and the respectful care they received was yet another model for how the natural world was to be honored for its partnership with humanity. The deep forest held dangerous predators with great spiritual power that were best left alone. Landscape features informed daily activities, and just as certain areas of the forest were avoided for their dangers, caves were critical places where humans could recreate creation events. The delicate balance of large human populations in a tropical landscape was maintained through personal and collective rituals that reinforced the value of careful attention to nature. Through cave offerings to the rain deities, or agricultural prayers to earth guardians, Maya people perpetuated a conversation with the forces of the natural world and reminded themselves how to live carefully.

Suggested Readings

Anderson, E. N., and Felix Medina Tzuc 2005 *Animals and the Maya in Southeast Mexico*. Tucson: University of Arizona Press.

Ford, Anabel, and Ronald Nigh 2015 *The Maya Forest Garden: Eight Millennia of Sustainable Cultivation of the Tropical Woodlands*. New York: Routledge.

Lucero, Lisa 2006 *Water and Ritual: The Rise and Fall of Classic Maya Rulers*. Austin: University Press of Texas.

Prufer, Keith, and James Brady, eds. 2005 *Stone Houses and Earth Lords: Maya Religion in the Cave Context*. Boulder: University Press of Colorado.

Re Cruz, Alicia 1996 *The Two Milpas of Chan Kom*. Albany: State University of New York Press.

Taube, Karl 2003 Ancient and Contemporary Maya Conceptions about Field and Forest. In *The Lowland Maya Area: Three Millennia at the Human-Wildland Interface*, ed. A. Gomez-Pompa et al., pp. 461–492. New York: Food Products Press.

4

Into the City

The landscape in Classic Maya times was a patchwork of large areas of sparsely settled agricultural production interspersed with chaotic and sprawling urban centers of varying size. Urbanism has been long debated in Maya studies but is usefully defined as a measure of geographical size, density of occupation, and range of social differentiation.[1] Much of what we know about ancient Maya culture comes from the investigation of large cities (anywhere from 3 to 60 square kilometers of settlement with populations estimated to be from 5,000 to 60,000 people at a time)[2] where elites ruled and daily life was filled with the spectacle and hardship to be found in any city. Crowded and noisy, but cleaner and more beautiful than the ancient cities of Europe according to firsthand accounts by Spanish explorers, each Maya city was unique. There was no template for how a city was designed, and they grew in what appears to be a haphazard manner, according to the changing fortunes of their leaders and economies. Recently, the idea of "low-density, agro-urbanism" has been applied to Maya cities, and they may have grown according to the environmental and farming potential of different neighborhoods. This would be an energy-efficient way to produce food close to consumers, especially in the absence of wheeled transport or pack animals.[3] As in all cities, a

[1] Hutson 2016:17.
[2] Hutson 2016:41–52.
[3] Isendahl 2012:1123.

great diversity of activities took place on a daily basis – from marketing to construction to performance. Literacy was available to some members of Maya urban centers. It was practiced by scribes and other professionals who studied how to write complicated hieroglyphic inscriptions, by craftspeople who carved texts into stone or wood, and by the members of royal families who consulted books and commissioned monuments to celebrate their accomplishments. Maya cities had ball courts, a central institution of elite culture where men competed against rivals in a reenactment of a mythological cycle that encapsulated the core values of Maya people. New research shows Maya cities had central markets where the goods and crafts produced in small households described in earlier chapters were exchanged or bartered among all levels of society. Often seen as an urban culture, it was the interplay of rural and urban that made city life possible.

AN URBAN LANDSCAPE

In the largest ancient Maya cities, such as Coba, on which this book is modeled, it might have taken more than two days to walk from one end of the urban sprawl to another (Figure 4.1). Some Maya cities were more than 60 square kilometers in size, when the dense urban core of monumental architecture and its surrounding residential compounds, fields, defensive features, and farming settlements are considered. Archaeologists estimate that many such cities held between 50,000 and 100,000 people at their peak at this time. There were dozens of cities of this size during the Classic period, and hundreds of smaller cities. Often smaller cities were located on hilltops, along a river, or at some other calculated location and made good use of the natural topography for palaces, temples, and residential areas. Maya cities do not appear at first glance to have been built with site planning principles, but when the topography is considered, it is clear that small and large cities emerged strategically (Figure 4.2). The family household compound discussed in Chapter 2 might have been a day's walk from the center of the city, but similar settlements were also closer to the center than that, given that the majority of the population of Maya cities were farmers of modest means, who produced enough

Into the City 71

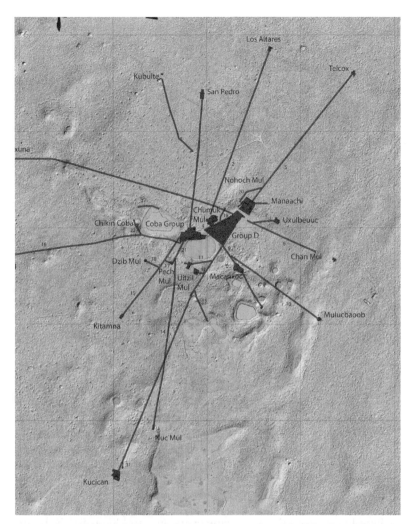

FIGURE 4.1 Lidar imagery of the very large ancient lakeside city of Coba, in Quintana Roo, Mexico. Pyramids, palace, and market areas are clustered in the center of the city, and roads radiate out to large residential groups likely controlled by important lineages. Small houses fill in almost all open areas. Image/map by Travis Stanton and courtesy of the Proyecto Yaxuna-Coba Sacbe.

surplus to support a small royal court with attached specialists. Even just a few hours' walk in any direction from downtown the landscape was filled with small houses, gardens, and agricultural fields.

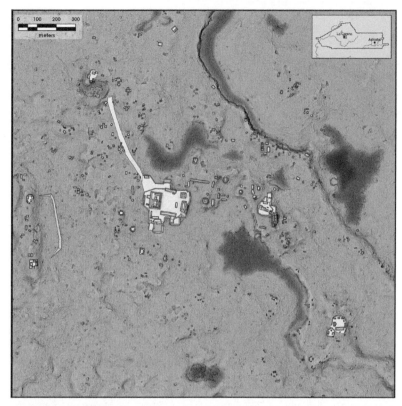

FIGURE 4.2 Map of central La Corona, built with lidar data that reveals natural topography with architectural features hand digitized. Lidar has transformed the mapping of ancient Maya settlements that are often buried under a millennia of forest growth. Map/Image by Marcello A. Canuto, courtesy of the La Corona Regional Project.

People traversed this landscape every day, and likely Sak Kab', the grandmother from a farming family without young children of her own to supervise, was sent on the journey into the city periodically to exchange goods the family made in the market, to look for a rare commodity that was available only from traders, or to serve the court in some manner. A particularly skilled weaver or cook might be summoned from a rural settlement to the palace at the behest of a queen who needed new royal garments or assistance with a diplomatic feast. A farmer with extra beeswax candles might travel into the city to trade these precious commodities for medicine or mineral pigments that came from far away. Leaving their homes with a ball of corn masa to eat along the way, these travelers would follow paths that ran alongside the massive paved white roads that emanated from the center of many Maya cities. Only certain people could travel on the roads themselves, walking on the smooth paved surfaces high above the ground, but everyone could follow alongside the roads, on the well-worn paths that existed before the roads were built. These white roads, or sacbe, had foundations of large square stones that held crushed rock and stone. They were covered with a flat plaster surface that made moving from the middle of the city out to the suburbs a quick and easy process for the king or his bureaucrats who came to collect tribute. Roads traversed the rocky terrain of the Yucatan peninsula and even crossed rejolladas, or natural sinkholes filled with rich soils used for agriculture, when the need arose. Rejolladas were valuable features of the landscape; usually dry sinkholes that formed in the weak limestone landscape, they accumulated soil over time and were excellent places to plant tree crops. Some rejolladas had fresh water wells at the base, which made them even more productive places to grow crops. Communities with many rejolladas generally had better agricultural yields and could grow crops to trade like cacao, which was difficult to grow in areas without deep soil. Territories were mapped by the construction and maintenance of road systems, and even after they fell into disrepair, these monumental creations were a constant reminder of the ability of the royalty to command the resources and manpower for huge construction projects.

As our travelers moved farther from their simple homes and closer to the heart of the city, the buildings they passed began to change. They could see the tops of the largest pyramids at the heart of the city, poking over the trees. Most of the travelers would never see those pyramids up close, as they were in areas only the noble families could visit. Houses were larger and had higher stone walls. Some had stone roofs rather than thatch, which made them very dark inside. Like the houses they passed on their way to the cornfields every day, these buildings were built on low platforms to protect their residents from flooding during the rainy season. The more elaborate residential groups still had gardens interspersed among the structures, and the outer edges of the city were filled with economically important tree crops such as ramon, avocado, and even the precious cacao, which may have been grown only by courtly arborists. More and more as they approached the city the households were surrounded by stone or border walls of cactus that separated one extended family group from another as the settlement density increased. Our travelers were thankful that walls were not necessary to mark and defend the land they held at their homes. Sometimes a narrow passageway was left between the stone walls, which intersected from the pathway along the sacbe, and it was clear that people who lived in this neighborhood walked down this passageway and shared the same path into the city. Many cities had defensive features that were much more elaborate than cactus house-lot walls. If the city was not built next to a series of lakes, like Coba, or on a high escarpment, like Waka' in modern Guatemala (and sometimes even if its location did take advantage of a naturally defensive location), the central settlement could be protected by a boundary wall. Most of these walls are not very tall, but they provided a foundation for prickly and dangerous plant material (like those cacti). Boundary walls could also have been staffed with warriors or others who enforced the message of territorial protection such walls symbolized. These types of construction became more common later in the Classic period, when warfare increased and resources were stretched thin.

As the architecture changed, so too did the people. Not everyone in the city was a farmer; most people likely had a household garden but there were plenty of skilled tradespeople who had responsibilities other than producing corn, beans, and squash. The architects who designed these complex vaulted buildings directed masons who stood on scaffolding to erect tall walls. Engineers who managed the water systems for the city made sure clay- and stone-lined pools held the rainwater they collected and that this water made it to the palace and royal compounds. They also managed the fish, algae, and other important resources from the five lakes that surrounded the city of Coba. Artists of all kinds were available to plait hair, create a tattoo, or trade for a new set of sandals. Craftspeople were busily carrying their ceramic pots and shell beads toward the center of the city, and priests and priestesses dedicated to a wide array of deities wandered about as they moved from temple to temple. Even people who did not speak Maya, traders and artists, made their way about the city center.

Into the City 75

Everyone knew that at the end of the largest sacbe was a wide open area where the urban market was found. Anyone could visit the market, as long as you brought something to exchange. People from the countryside would travel in with honey, beeswax, or smoked peccary meat. People from the suburbs would bring the pottery they had found on their journeys to another nearby city, or perhaps a new style of figurine. If you were lucky there might be a trader with exotic stones on display such as jade or pyrite. Jade came in many different shades of green, and while the brightest apple-green and rare blue-green stones were reserved for the royalty, if one found a hungry trader who needed a bowl of stew or a bean tamale, even a simple person could trade for a small bead of dark green jadeite or serpentine, a green stone relative of jade. Pyrite, the iron-rich mineral with a metallic luster, was even more rare but not as popular. It was interesting to see one's reflection in the mirrors made of small mosaic pieces of pyrite, but very few people sought out the trader for this material in comparison with life-giving jade. There were always people with obsidian, the razor-sharp volcanic glass that everyone needed for cutting twine, hides, and almost anything else. Obsidian was only found far to the south of the city, many days' walk, and most citizens would never travel to this southern land where the language was different. But because it was the absolutely best material for cutting, full-time traders moved obsidian from the south to the cities of the northern Maya area on a more or less full-time basis. In a huge city like Coba, one could always find an obsidian trader who had just arrived from the coast with goods. In the smaller cities farther inland, it was less certain you could find the perfect tool for your task.

The analysis of obsidian artifacts has played a central role in the history of Maya archaeology. Given its importance as a daily tool or commodity, and the very few sources, the study of how obsidian was exchanged has helped scholars understand the interdependence of the Maya lowlands and highlands, as well as regions of Mesoamerica beyond the Maya area. From a single obsidian fragment, an archaeologist can discern what type of tool an ancient person used, and from abrasions and residues left on the fragment we can identify the types of activities it helped an ancient person perform. For example, if the obsidian blade was a ceremonial tool, it might have traces of human blood remaining on the surface, which could be seen under a microscope. If the obsidian was used to cut plant fibers for weaving into baskets or mats, it would likely have a particular sheen that results from the abrasion of the plant material against the hard obsidian surface. From that same fragment, an archaeologist could through visual or compositional analysis identify where the obsidian originated. Perhaps it came from the Maya highlands in Guatemala or from the central Basin of Mexico near modern-day Mexico City – two areas separated by thousands of kilometers from the northern Maya lowlands where Coba is located. By tracking which source was more popular at which time, and at which ancient city, archaeologists have begun to notice patterns in obsidian trade that likely derive from political alliances. An artifact made of green obsidian from central Mexico suggests ties with non-Maya traders, who moved items out of central Mexico and along the Gulf of Mexico. An artifact of gray or black obsidian suggests trade connections with the major polities of the southern Maya lowlands that dominated most Maya trade routes in the Classic period. Thus one obsidian fragment can be a powerful window into ancient Maya life – and excavation can yield thousands of obsidian artifacts.

The market was a loud and exciting place where much more than material goods were exchanged. Many people came to visit and share gossip or to try to hear the latest political news about the royal family and their wars of expansion. Vendors who provided tattoos, hair braiding, or dental work traded their skills for products they needed. Animals escaped their wicker pens and the smell of warm tamales and spicy stews wafted through the crowds. Only the most minimal structures separated one vendor from another – small rows of stone that were easily moved by a vendor greedy for more space. Trash was everywhere – mostly fruit and vegetable peelings from the food that people ate at the market, but also tamale wrappers, butchered animal waste, and broken fiber baskets. All of this was swept to the sides of the market each evening in preparation for the next day. Many women would bring the same kind of fruit to market – when mamey fruit was in season, a dozen vendors would all have mamey, but each woman had her own argument about why her fruit was best. People spent time visiting and debating the merits of the food they wanted to buy, looking for someone who wanted what they had to exchange and trying to get the best deal. They stopped to try fruit juice from one vendor and a spicy vegetable stew from another. These social interactions were a key way in which information flowed through the urban population – for example, those who lived close to the palace would share the gossip of who in the royal family was sick or ailing. Those who lived on the borderlands with the neighboring polity would tell stories of the advancement of the rival king or queen. The social life of the market was a fundamental experience of what it meant to be an urban citizen. Vendors would take pride in the number of people who visited their stalls, which was nearly as important as the profit they made since each visitor brought with them new information and a larger social network. In the Classic period, ancient Maya people did not use a standardized currency, although certain items like salt or cacao beans may have been so universally valued that they achieved a nearly currency-like status. Both items had the inherent advantage of being able to be divisible into nearly infinitely smaller quantities as negotiations evolved.

After nightfall those who had not made the long walk back to their homes in the suburbs or surrounding rural settlement might camp on the edge of the market space overnight and wait for whatever spectacle might take place in the city that night. The large open spaces of markets provided a place where people gathered for dancing and ceremonies. At night these were lit with torches, and costumed dancers from one of the temples would perform a ceremony that anyone could witness. On high holy days the priests would take part, or if a new king had been born or taken the throne, a ceremony to mark this special occasion would certainly be performed on the steps of one of the largest and most important pyramid temples. But on a daily basis, once the marketplace had quieted down and been swept clean, city people gathered to experience the social life of the city. Musicians would play drums or bone flutes; traders would tell stories of the strange places they visited and the cold mountains or scorching salt flats. People who provided services to repair a broken ceramic pot or fashion a set of leather sandals would wander the open area making themselves available to citizens and visitors. Healers and charlatans would promise to cure wounds that would not heal or eyes that were failing. Beggars, escaped slaves, and criminals would attempt to blend in with the crowd. The city was ever-changing and provided a space for everyone.

FIGURE 4.3 View of the nearby lake system from the top of the pyramidal structure known as Nohoch Mul, the tallest pyramid at Coba. Photograph by the author.

From the large marketplace and gathering area it was easy to view the most impressive architecture of the city. One of the most characteristic features of ancient Maya cities are the large pyramids seemingly placed randomly across the landscape (Figure 4.3). Many of these were over 20 meters in height and all were topped with a small temple at the summit. On special occasions like the inauguration of a ruler or the completion of a calendar cycle, priests were carried to the top of these steep pyramids in a litter decorated with brightly colored flags and standards. From this vantage point a priestess sang or spoke to the crowds below her, chanting or praying for assistance from the gods and ancestors of her dynasty. From painted ceramic vases and graffiti we know these performers were dressed in all the regalia of their office, including large headdresses of brilliantly colored feathers that were visible to even those on the edges of the plaza below. Incense burners billowing scented smoke, placed on the steps in front of temples, added to the dramatic effect. Many of these pyramids were funerary markers for distinguished kings and queens – monuments they designed themselves and whose construction took place over the course of their lifetimes. Deep within these pyramids are their royal tombs, built to recreate the mythic origin of Maya people from the mist-shrouded mountains of the highlands. Some of the tombs were accessible via labyrinths and passageways from the surface of the pyramid, while others were designed to be left open for a period of time until it was the right moment to complete the pyramid construction, and then the tombs were sealed forever. These impressive monuments were built with the labor of city dwellers, most of whom did not have a choice about whether or not they participated in these massive construction projects, but all of whom were told it was an essential part of being from a royal kingdom. Built with local stone, often on top of earlier structures, the pyramids of artistically inclined or spiritually devout royalty were covered in carved stucco decoration that might be painted bright red with hematite-infused pigment. These decorations transformed the plain stone temple into the sacred earth monster mountain of Maya mythology, and provided a way for the ruling family to place themselves at the center of these origin stories.

As one wandered the downtown area of ancient Maya cities on any given day there were many architectural wonders in addition to the pyramids. Large paved roads crisscrossed the city leading from the center to important suburbs where bureaucrats and second-level elites lived. Large wells with stone-lined borders and other water storage features such as underground chambers or shallow stone-lined pools for collecting rainwater were common. At least one ball court, but sometimes more, with parallel buildings and a paved playing surface could be found near the palace compounds of the royalty. Smaller temples dedicated to calendar rites and gathering houses for young men to learn the arts of diplomacy and war were also found in the center. Smaller buildings that housed the wealthier members of the city were wedged in and around these impressive architectural features. The best locations were reserved for dynastic royal palaces, and there may have been more than one of these given that the largest Maya cities had rival dynasties in constant competition for the throne.

LITERACY

Also common within the public areas of ancient Maya cities were tall stone stelae, or monuments carved to commemorate the divine rulers of Maya civilization. These 2-meter or taller megaliths served as both public art and state propaganda, conveying a message of the power of the royalty to control their own depictions, to monopolize skilled artisans, and especially to convey meaning through text. Each stela usually had a life-sized (or even larger) portrait of a king or queen, dressed in their royal finery and often holding the key regalia of their office, as they did when rituals of state were performed in front of their citizens. These portraits were surrounded, in most cases, with a long hieroglyphic text that recorded in detail the life history and accomplishments of the person depicted, the accomplishments of their family, or, in some cases, their entire dynastic line. Because of their very restricted use – hieroglyphs are only found in elite contexts such as on stela, on items placed in tombs, and within the private temples of the elite – scholars have concluded that literacy was not widespread in ancient Maya times. Of our travelers to the city, perhaps only Sak Kab' could understand a small part of the hieroglyphic texts carved on stelae. The majority of people who moved through the city every day recognized writing for its ability to convey information but could not discern the meaning of the text.[4] To them, it was something reserved for the elite. Because our rural grandmother spent time in the market, and had made friends there with women vendors of all classes, she understood how the Maya numerical system worked – a dot represented the number 1, and bars meant 5 – these symbols could combine in an infinite number of ways to convey quantity. When visiting the city she would often stop to look at the stone stelae and find the bars and dots scattered throughout the text. Even though she was fairly certain the text did not have to do with economic

[4] Houston and Stuart 1992.

Into the City

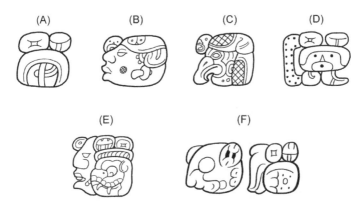

FIGURE 4.4 Examples of six different methods available to write the ajaw title, which is read today as "lord" or "ruler," in Classic period Maya hieroglyphics. (A) Graphic form, (B) portrait of the Maize Deity Juun Ajaw, (C) vulture form, (D) day sign form spelling k'uhul ajaw, "holy lord," (E) with the female prefix ix as "lady snake lord," and (F) with the young prefix as "young Piedras Negras lord." Illustration by Simon Martin.

transactions, she was not at all clear what it described. From the images of the king and queen near the text she knew it had to do with the most powerful and holy occupants of the city. And she could pick out powerful animals that appeared as miniature logographs in the text – a monkey here, a parrot there. Sak Kab' admired the fluid skill of the scribes and stone carvers, and to her, the stela was a monument to the immense intelligence and power of her city's leaders.

Classic Maya written language was very complex and almost any idea could be expressed in written form in a number of ways – through logograms as in the modern Chinese writing system, through pictographs as in Egyptian hieroglyphs, through phonetic elements as in our own writing system, or in a combination of these three approaches (Figure 4.4). The relative consistency and complexity of Maya inscriptions across the lowlands during the Classic period argues for schools of instruction – places where young royalty not destined for the throne were sent to learn not only how to write but also the art of conveying meaning through text. In painted imagery from the Classic period we find a deity of scribes that takes the form of a howler monkey, one of the largest monkeys of the New World, and one of the most clever and imposing creatures of the Maya rainforest – their cries can be heard for over 5 kilometers! The Maya monkey god was a

FIGURE 4.5 Monkey god of writing, patron of artists on a Classic period ceramic vase. Photo: University of Miami Special Collections, Jay I. Kislak Collection.

major patron of the arts who helped shape the first people (Figure 4.5). Scholars have discovered a lingua franca of Maya, now extinct, that was used in the vast majority of inscriptions and that differed in certain ways from spoken Maya of the Classic period.[5] Maya inscriptions are famous for the use of puns and double entendre, sophisticated witticisms that required an advanced education to appreciate. At certain historical moments, literate traditions were so refined that scribes wrote complicated glyphic inscriptions in

---

[5] Houston et al. 2000.

mirror image or ordered the glyph blocks in a counterclockwise spiral, just to display their skill in the use and performance of text. These tricks of hand emphasize how profoundly writing was used to convey and reinforce relationships of power and inequality. Given the choices available to Maya scribes for how to write information, they had the ability to make their meaning more or less obscure, to speak to a larger or more exclusive audience, and thus to reinforce the highly specialized nature of reading and writing.

During any given day in a large Maya city, there were many skilled artisans who collaborated with these highly trained scribes to create the public and private art that utilized textual passages. Stonemasons hauled the huge stone stelae from quarries many kilometers outside the city to the central precinct where likely a different group of stone craftspeople took over the intricate carving of dynastic histories and royal portraiture. Stelae almost always celebrate the accomplishments of the queens and kings of powerful dynasties. They were commissioned by the royalty and created to glorify their distinguished ancestors or their endeavors to protect the city through ritual and war. Similar stone panels were also commissioned for certain more private areas of royal palaces and tombs, such as over the doorways or as part of a chamber wall, but many stone monuments were meant to be viewed by a wide audience of citizens, even if most of those people grasped only the physical and visual impact of a huge stone tree planted in the middle of the city. Writing was also deployed in other media such as on painted books and ceramic vessels, which were created by scribes and artisans within the palace compounds. These were much more private and esoteric texts, meant for the truly literate members of society. Painted bark-paper books contained calendrical and astronomical information that told the fortune of auspicious and inauspicious days; painted texts on cylindrical pots often commemorated the visits between elites and their privileged access to the complexities of Maya mythology. Almost all surviving examples of Classic Maya writing are finished texts; however, at the 9th-century site of Xultun, one room of the palace has mathematical calculations carved into, and painted upon, the plaster of an interior wall.[6] The

---

[6] Saturno et al. 2012.

calculations are at eye level if one is sitting cross-legged on the floor, and provide us with a rare example of the immense amount of time and effort that went into mastering Maya writing and calendrical calculations. Repeated plastering shows the scribes created blank slates for more calculations rather than reaching for a new piece of bark paper or scratching the numbers in a wax tablet.

As with the experience of hieroglyphic writing, most visitors to the city would have been familiar with the most important holidays and auguries of the calendar, but the more detailed and obscure movements of the planets recorded on stelae were the province of other court specialists. Recording and predicting the movement of the planets as well as the sun and moon were key components of the Maya system of time measurement. The first appearance of Venus as an evening star was something many families noticed during the quiet evenings in the countryside, but within the city, highly trained astronomers and astrologers kept track of the annual cycles of Mercury, Mars, Venus, and possibly Jupiter. They could predict solar and lunar eclipses, as well as the equinoxes and solstices. This sophisticated observational astronomy, coupled with a flexible numerical system, made an elaborate system of interlocking calendars possible. The most important of these calendars were the Long Count and the Calendar Round. The Long Count was a single record of elapsed time since August 14, 3114 BCE – a moment well before Maya culture had emerged as a distinct entity and thus a mythical time tied to the origin of the world. The Calendar Round was a 52-year count comprised of the synchronization of a 260-day cycle and a 365-day cycle. The 365-day cycle, or haab, was based on the solar year, with 18 months of 20 days each and an additional five holy days at the end of the cycle.

The 260-day cycle, or tzolkin, was used throughout ancient Mesoamerica as the holy calendar for divination and the timing of religious events. It is comprised of 20 day names with the numbers 1 through 13, to create 260 unique day/name combinations. The tzolkin is so meaningful to Maya people that it continues to be used today in the Guatemalan highlands, more than 2,500 years since its earliest documented appearance. Modern divination priests keep track of the 260-day calendar and use it to predict auspicious times for planting corn, building a house, or holding a wedding. As with other systems of astrology, it is also used to divine the fortune of a child, their future character, and an ensuing appropriate name. The tzolkin cycle of 260 days has many layers of significance within Maya culture, as it is also the length of time from a woman's first missed menstrual period to the birth of a child, the length of corn agricultural cycles in the Maya highlands, and the length of time Venus is visible as a morning star. Given its pervasive use throughout Mesoamerica, and its survival after the imposition of European systems of time management, it is likely the daily lives of most Classic Maya people were orchestrated according to the tzolkin.

BALL GAMES AND ROYAL RESPONSIBILITY

Although grandmother Sak Kab' was free to conduct trade in the marketplace and to wander the open plazas to admire stelae and temples, there were places within the city she was not permitted to visit. Everyone from the countryside knew the palace and its associated kitchens and patios were private areas for the royal family, and unless one was summoned by an emissary of the court no one would try to enter those places. Likewise for an elderly woman, there were places that were inappropriate for her to visit such as the men's houses and ball courts – these were settings for urban boys and men to socialize and perform the rituals of masculinity that solidified their place of importance within Maya society, not as farmers or fathers, but as warriors and ball players. The men's houses were large, open buildings where the male youth of the city – those whose families did not need them to work in the fields or to make stone tools or pottery – went to spend time in the company of other men. They trained physically to be accomplished warriors, and importantly they trained socially in the skills that men were expected to perform, as well as in the appropriate bearing. They spent years in each other's company and formed close friendships that would prove useful when they left the men's house and started a family. Those whose wives were about to give birth would return to the men's house for a time, and mentor the younger ones. Games like patolli, where pebbles or other tokens were moved around a board, were played on the wide-open platforms of the men's house, just as they were played in the rural households, and young men learned how to wield spears and master hand-to-hand combat in the patio areas.

Full-scale war with military regiments was rare in Classic Maya times, but defending the city from raids and especially escorting the queen and king when they traveled to another polity was a daily responsibility of the security forces drawn from mid-level elites. We do not have any surviving evidence of a standing military order or large barracks and warehouses found in other ancient cultures that mounted a full-time military. To date, archaeologists have not discovered a "killing field" or other evidence of massive military loss of life. Yet there is substantial imagery of conflict, including groups of warriors, bound captives, as well as the defensive works mentioned earlier, evidence of burned structures and entire neighborhoods, abandoned cities, and human skeletons with evidence of prolonged exposure to trauma. According to the written records Maya royalty left on stelae and palace panels, warfare was recurring, but not continual.[7] Cities, rulers, and polities differed in how much they utilized military imagery in their official art and presumably how much they engaged in martial activity. Our knowledge of the great alliances made at the height of the Classic period has advanced to the point where we know many of the cities under the protection of the most politically powerful of all Maya cities, Calakmul, did not engage in warfare or battles among themselves for hundreds of years. Alliance with the great powers of Calakmul or Tikal may have been motivated by the desire to avoid war, or it may have provided the resources necessary to intimidate neighboring territories into a begrudging peace. The warrior ideal was "woven into the fabric of Classic Maya kingship"[8] and hieroglyphic statements make it obvious that proclamations about success in war and captive taking were understood not only as a reflection of the skill of the king but as an indication of the spiritual health and security of the entire polity. Ancestors with military accomplishments were often invoked by their descendants, and the success of any individual king in the arena of war was seen to be in part the result of his ancestral inheritance and dynastic gods.

While kings and other elite men trained in battle and were equipped with padded armor, shields, spears, clubs, knives, axes, rock slings, and blowguns with poison tips, these specialists were augmented by

[7] Martin 2020:229.
[8] Martin 2020:228.

FIGURE 4.6 Ceramic figurine of a warrior with shield and skull necklace. Photo: Lowe Art Museum 86.0033.

commoners who had little more than knives and their wits (Figure 4.6). It is unclear to scholars how often commoners were required to go into battle, and if they participated in raids for captives, but by Postclassic times we have evidence that military actions by groups of commoners increased when necessary. Royals may have considered the agricultural season when they deliberated about how many commoners they could conscript, and Simon Martin has shown that inscriptions demonstrate that warfare events were most common in the dry season, when planting and harvesting activities were completed.[9] Classic period

---

[9] Martin 2020:224.

painted vases often show groups of warriors presenting captives to kings, along with some of the goods they may have raided from neighboring palaces, including bundles of cotton cloth, baskets of beans or corn, feathers, and pelts – all items that commoners had to provide to their royal families in tribute. Thus Maya warfare had an economic component, and some scholars suggest conflict was often motivated by desire for more subjects who could provide tribute rather than for more territory, although the two often went hand in hand.[10] High-status captives could be ransomed or forced to concede tribute, and captive lands populated with commoners could be forced to deliver tribute items to a victor. In both cases, a military success might have made a royal family prosperous. Given that cities victorious in war often experienced a building and construction boom immediately following the defeat of an enemy, war also may have included the removal of a rival's architects, stonemasons, and engineers as a form of intellectual plunder. Likewise, the looting of a rival's ancestral bundles or other prized ceremonial items was cause for great anguish as it allowed the defacement of these living, breathing entities, or their manipulation toward the fortunes of the victor and away from protecting and aiding their rightful owners.

Rulers traveled in caravans, often carried on litters, in order to visit subordinate towns and receive tribute, attend negotiations to maintain their alliances, or participate in the rituals associated with the installment of a new queen or king. Even the rulers of minor dynasties were vulnerable to capture, as one important way for young Maya kings to distinguish themselves was to seize and display their peers from rival polities. This activity became part of the titles they carried in hieroglyphic statements – Bird Jaguar IV of Yaxchilan is known as "He of Twenty Captives" on many monuments. Some kings who were abducted were later returned to their thrones as vassals of their captors. Their value was too great as an ongoing source of tribute or wealth to simply receive a single ransom payment. Women were rarely taken captive in war, or at least few hieroglyphic texts describe the ransom or display of royal women. However, some scholars have

---

[10] Martin 2020:232.

pointed out that marriage alliances, which were hardly consensual on the part of female participants, often were negotiated in a manner that had military implications. Outside the safety of a palace, royals were at risk not only of capture but of having their royal jewels and other objects of power stolen. This humiliation was borne by not only the king or queen but by their entire kingdom. It signaled an ominous turn of fortune for a semi-divine ruler to be violated in this manner, so security was paramount, and caravans traveled with trusted and trained guards. At other times these trained security forces were called upon to accompany a king or queen when they orchestrated such a raid on a rival dynasty. Under cover of night, the ruler and their regiment would ambush their enemies, capturing the highest-ranking member of the family, and then return with that poor captive to their home city. Unlucky royals in this situation were displayed for all of the urban population to ridicule, stripped of their royal finery and bound with hands behind their back. Often a ransom would be demanded for their release, but in some cases they were held captive, tortured, or sacrificed. A king who was particularly aggressive would aim to capture the skilled astronomers and scribes of his opponent, leaving the dynasty without the ability to divine the movement of the planets or communicate royal accomplishments.[11] These were spiritual crises to be avoided at all costs, and thus trained security forces drawn from the children of loyal families were essential protection for elite power. The elite likely formed close relationships with some of their security forces, and it appears that royal queens who were in line for the throne took non-royal but highly distinguished soldiers as their marriage partners on more than one occasion.

The ball game was played by these same young men. Occasionally, the king would dress in the full uniform and equipment of a master sportsman, or the queen would throw out the opening ball, but the actual play was done by members of the upper classes who did not stand in line to the throne and thus could risk the injury the game involved. We know the game was a preoccupation of the elite since it is often depicted on the painted cylindrical vases they exchanged with one another and that provide an excellent source of information to us

---

[11] Johnston 2001.

FIGURE 4.7 Ball game yoke, or belt, made of polished limestone and decorated with imagery of the dying Maize Deity. Photo: Lowe Art Museum 2004.70.3.

today. It required extensive physical training, as once the ball was put into play it was never supposed to stop moving. The players, usually only two men, were allowed to hit the solid rubber ball with their elbows, thighs, head – any part but their hands. They wore thick cotton clothing that protected them from the impact of the ball to some degree, but they also wore heavy stone yokes, or belts, that made the game even more difficult. Many of these stone belts have been found archaeologically and are now in museum collections – they are often decorated with underworld symbolism that reinforces how the Classic period ball game was related to the descent of the Hero Twins into the underworld (Figure 4.7). Some scholars have suggested these belts were not worn during play but were akin to the championship belt awarded a boxer or wrestler today. Balls would careen off the sloped sides of the courts, and hit or pass through a hoop at the top of each structure. The men would run to keep up with the ball and hit it toward their opponent until they were sweating and exhausted (Figure 4.8). The game was played with only a few spectators – other men who were in training, those royals who were patrons of the players, and perhaps a child or two who hid behind the corner of

Into the City

FIGURE 4.8 Ballplayers in traditional uniform engaged in play with a large rubber ball along the steps of a ball court. Photo by Justin Kerr, K4407, Dumbarton Oaks, Trustees for Harvard University, Washington. University of Miami Special Collections, Jay I. Kislak Collection.

the ball court without being noticed. Everyone nearby could hear the smack of rubber against hard limestone when a player hit the ball forcefully against the walls of the court. It gave out a loud clap, just like thunder. The hard rubber ball, made from sap of a local tree that was boiled down until it could be stretched and molded into a sphere, often had an object placed at the center – a powerful stone, shell, or even the skull of an ancestor who had excelled at the game. The king had a ball with his own grandfather's skull inside, but it was never used for actual play.

Ball games were played often in the rural and outlying settlement of Coba, but less frequently in the city. Each of the major royal compounds had a ball court, since each king wanted to lay claim to the ability to order the universe and seasons through this sacred game. Within the urban core, the ball game was played on special calendrical occasions like the winter solstice and the start of the rainy season, and it was important that a new king play the game successfully before he was inaugurated.[12] This was because the king and the entire royal dynasty were responsible for the perpetuation of life – the life of their city, the life of their people, and the life of the cornfields that sustained Maya culture. Playing the ball game with skill demonstrated

[12] Gillespie 1991.

how seriously the king took his responsibility to understand the movements of the sun, the moon, and the seasons. Whether he played the game or it was played by his champion, the ballplayer reenacted the responsibility of the royal family to ensure successful harvests, to foster the fertility and growth of their subjects, and to defend the land of the polity from threats of any kind, whether they be drought, plague, or invasion. Knowing and tracking the movements of the planets was key to fulfilling these tasks, and that is why the royal court contained astrologers and astronomers – but knowing when the seasons would change and when the rains would come was only part of the equation. Demonstrating the king's willingness to endure hardship and pain in order to fulfill this responsibility was communicated powerfully in the ball game, when elite men took direct blows from a miniaturized version of the sun in order to ensure balance and regularity in the universe. Their sacrifice made possible the return of the rains after the long dry season when the earth appeared to be on the brink of death. It made possible the growth of crops, people, and animals. When a visiting royal man performed more skillfully on the ball court than the resident players, people whispered that he might be a more powerful advocate for their welfare, or his ancestors offered greater protection against death. Given the importance of the ball game as a way to perform elite male skill and royal responsibility, the ball game was often depicted in elite art and took on great political significance as a reflection of the power of the dynasty. Kings were depicted playing the game in the underworld, even after their death, because they continued to influence the world of the living and fulfill their responsibilities to family dynasties. Powerful mothers and grandmothers are depicted throwing out the first ball or summoning famous ancient ballplayers to compete against the disruptive gods of the underworld. From images on ceramic vases and carved stone monuments we know that death was no limitation on royal responsibility, and those who excelled in the performance of the royal duties in life would likely remain busy in the underworld defending their subjects against threats and ensuring an orderly world for the living.

Because so much of the research into ancient Maya culture has been done inside royal cities, most people think of Maya culture as urban, although not as densely urban as ancient Rome or Tenochtitlan. And it is true that many aspects of urban life were key components of what we know as Classic Maya culture: the elaborate temples and architecture of ancient cities, the raised roads and carved stone monuments, and especially the tombs and palaces of the elite were all clustered in urban spaces. But without a huge supporting population of farmers who produced surplus food, urban life would have come to a standstill. Indeed, the final blow to Classic Maya cities of the southern lowlands that left them empty when Europeans arrived in the 16th century was the decision of the supporting population to pick up and move away from the city. An occasional weak king could be endured during the millennia of Maya urban life, but a loss of faith in the urban way of life devastated Maya culture and ushered in an entirely new era in the Postclassic period. Hundreds of years earlier, when cities were thriving, markets were filled with goods from throughout not only the Maya lowlands but other regions of Mesoamerica. People exchanged news and ideas as goods changed hands. Complex literate traditions flourished and royalty proclaimed their accomplishments on carved monuments for the urban population to see and appreciate, even if they were not able to read the details of the text. Men trained for war and the more common need for defense, as well as for the competitive sporting events that provided another avenue for the resolution of conflict. The ball game was the most spiritually and politically significant of these arenas, and allowed elites to perform their role as guardians of the living world. Through their divinely granted benevolence, crops and people flourished or failed. Although often depicted as consumed with esoteric ritual, Maya rulers were deeply indebted to their supporting rural populations, and the interplay of both royal and commoner within the agricultural system is what allowed Maya society to endure.

Suggested Readings

Coe, Michael D., and Mark Van Stone 2001 *Reading the Maya Glyphs*. New York: Thames and Hudson.

Hutson, Scott R. 2016 *The Ancient Urban Maya: Neighborhoods, Inequality, and Built Form*. Gainesville: University Press of Florida.

King, Eleanor M. 2015 *The Ancient Maya Marketplace: The Archaeology of Transient Space*. Tucson: University of Arizona Press.

Scarborough, Vernon L., and David R. Wilcox, eds. 1991 *The Mesoamerican Ballgame*. Tucson: University of Arizona Press.

5

Palace Life

The major Maya cities of the Classic period all contain one or more palace compounds composed of numerous separate rooms linked by interior patios and courtyards. Difficult to access, they were private spaces for the royal extended family to practice courtly arts and enjoy the company of one another in safety. Excavation of a large palace complex at the powerful site of Calakmul provides artifactual evidence that different activities were conducted in each of the many rooms of the palace.[1] Lower terrace rooms were used for less important tasks, such as cooking and production of utilitarian stone tools, while the rooms on higher terraces were used for making more prestigious goods such as marine shell ornaments and cotton cloth. Artisans seem to have lived at the base of the palace complex and left few material objects, perhaps because they did not have access to goods other than basic provisions. In the largest cities the presence of more than one such palace compound underscores a persistent competition between dynasties that is also evident in hieroglyphic inscriptions commissioned by those elite who succeeded in taking the throne and installing their family in a secure position of power. Mirroring the lives of the majority of Maya people, the palaces had places for the preparation of food, for craft activities, and for sleeping and rest. But in contrast to most Maya families, the lives of the royalty were full of

---

[1] Folan 1992.

leisure, with their needs attended to by a large court of attendants, servants, and likely enslaved people (although the evidence for slavery is scant). This left them free to spend time in ritual, perfecting their artistic skills, or reading the almanacs or codices that predicted the nature of each day. Many hours were also spent entertaining visiting dignitaries, hosting feasts, and in private discussion with political allies. Most Classic Maya art depicts these activities, indicating how important it was for dynasties to commemorate the skillful participation of their members in such courtly arts. Diplomacy, the reckoning of time, and spiritual mediation were skills not only that elite members of society possessed but that royals needed to proclaim and display in order to reinforce their highly privileged status within society. It is certain that within Classic Maya society the majority of the population believed deeply in the semi-divine nature of their rulers, but it is also apparent that the rulers took great pains to reinforce this idea whenever possible.

SPIRITUAL MEDIATION

The oldest member of the royal family Ihk' Tis, or Black Tapir, awoke with a start just before dawn. No one else in the sleeping quarters of the royal family was awake, although the palace cooks had been busy for an hour at least, grinding fresh corn dough for hot pozole and mixing ripe fruit with water. The great uncle of the queen was a four katun lord (katun is the Maya word for a twenty-year period of time) over eighty years of age, and still in vibrant health – which made him unique within the kingdom, as far as anyone knew. Most of his close relatives had passed away decades ago. He thought about the exhausting night of spiritual battle he had just led. In his estimation, his ferocity as a spiritual avatar of the dynasty grew stronger as his physical strength waned. Today Ihk' Tis would spend much of the day in rest, preparing for another night of battle. While others slept, the great-uncle transformed into his unique wahy spirit (Figure 5.1) – a companion that could do battle with other powerful wahy spirits that frequented the night skies.[2]

---

[2] Houston and Stuart 1989.

FIGURE 5.1 Classic Codex-style vessel with three wahy spirits. Each faces a hieroglyphic caption that includes the wahy glyph, composed of an abstracted human face with one eye covered by jaguar skin. Photo: Maya, Codex-style vase with "wahy" figures, about 650–850 CE. Denver Art Museum: Gift of Dr. M. Larry and Nancy B. Ottis, 1998.424. Photograph courtesy of the Denver Art Museum.

While some dynasts had macaw parrot or jaguar wahy spirits, the wahy of the great-uncle was an even more fearsome supernatural creature that combined the most ferocious aspects of a tapir with the wily intelligence of a spider monkey. Tapirs were huge and muscular, and without fear could rush any creature of the forest, crushing them or ripping off a limb. Monkeys were tricksters, able to outwit opponents and solve any dilemma with their intelligence. He was very fortunate to have been born on a day when this wahy sought him out. It was a wahy spirit that his ancestors had known as well, and one day, he hoped a younger member of the dynasty would be born with the same powerful wahy to take over his night battles. His polity was strong, his city growing, but that was because he was vigilant about his work – every day he rested and every night while he appeared to sleep, he entered into the night sky to defend the economic and political prosperity of his kingdom. This tangible prosperity was the result of the dynasty's spiritual power.

When Ihk' Tis rose from the thick cotton mat where family members slept together under the watchful eye of their guards, he pulled back the gauzy curtain that led to the next room. The smooth plaster floor was cool on his feet and a guard came to help him to the altar. This was the room where the gods of the dynasty slept until they were needed for the ceremonial performances that his family executed for their kingdom. Like the sleeping chamber, this room was deep within the maze of palace rooms with only a single doorway from the hidden room where Ihk' Tis rested. Dynastic god images were sometimes stolen by thieves from a competing dynasty, such as other royalty who lived in the city but had lost favor and the throne, or even by outsiders from another region. If the figurines were stolen, rituals could not be performed, and the fate of the dynasty would certainly falter. He opened the polished wooden cabinet and saluted each of them in turn. All were made by members of his own family of the most precious hardwood from deep in the forest; such images were his closest companions these days (Figure 5.2). He tended them and knew they looked out for him as well. Some days Ihk' Tis offered them copal incense, and on other days he offered water from a sacred well located deep in the forest. When royal visitors from the south arrived at the palace, these images would be placed in the meeting room to convey the importance and longevity of his dynasty. When the queen went to war, as she was likely to do again soon, he would remove the images from this case and place them in her temple room so she could ask the gods of her dynasty for their assistance in her quest. She was the one who held the power to open the portal to messages from ancestral gods, but he was the one who spent time with the gods each and every day.

These precious objects, with their carefully made clothing and jewels, had also been brought into the light of day during the accession ceremony for Queen K'awiil Ajaw. City dwellers did not get to see these avatars very often, and they certainly never touched them or even got very close. That would disrupt the royal divine energy they held. But the accession of a king or queen was a momentous occasion with extensive and complicated ceremonies during which the dynastic gods were asked to witness the seating of the queen. Many people did not know how much effort was put into this ritual. They saw the grand regalia of office and the elaborate clothing of the royal family and were satisfied. Only other members of a court could understand the spiritual obligations that came with taking the throne, and how a queen and king begged their dynastic gods to show favor on the city and its territories. Without royal blood it was unlikely the gods would look on them favorably, and without lengthy prayers into the night,

FIGURE 5.2 Carved wooden deity figure. Photo: Unknown artist, Maya, Effigy Portrait of Ruler about 1032–1173 CE. Denver Art Museum: Gift of Mr. William I. Lee, 1985.649. Photograph courtesy of the Denver Art Museum.

their immediate ancestors might not remain close at hand and watch over the court. But this was the work his family, and his family only, was trained to do. As children, they witnessed diplomatic visits from their mother's knee where she sat outside the main meeting room. As a young man, he had participated in the accession of an earlier king and the all-night rituals it entailed.

The accession ceremonies of his niece consumed everyone in the royal palace compound for weeks. Preparations were extensive as the palace had to be cleaned and renovated, massive amounts of food prepared, and new robes and regalia made for all the officiants. Court astrologers recommended a date when Venus, after disappearing for days, would reappear magically as a morning star.[3] Given that the claim of the queen to the throne rested largely on her hugely successful military activities, this date was agreed upon by all the counselors. Days of pre-inauguration rituals included elaborate presentations to the whole city of captives from nearby royal families and performances by the court dancers who retold the mythological origin of the dynasty. A crocodile was captured in a net from the lakes – only royal fishermen went into the lakes – and kept in a cage near the temple where the accession eventually took place. Days of prayer and fasting in the royal palace and festivities in the city at large culminated at dawn on the winter solstice. The new queen would become the sun, and grow strong as the days grew longer, bright as the morning star. Once the ritual began, the new queen – dressed in yards and yards of long, flowing cloth embellished with designs that recalled her rightful place as the portal of her dynasty – performed all the highly scripted acts that the rulers of her city had done for centuries. She was carried on a litter up the steps of the temple to pray to the dynastic gods and ask them to be present for her accession to the throne. On the steps of the temple she let her own blood and offered it to her ancestors and the gods watching over the event. Priests handed her the holy regalia of rulership, the two-headed ceremonial bar made of rare wood from deep in the forest, and the scepter made of brilliant obsidian in the form of the rulership deity. Carried down from the top of the pyramid, she wore the carved wooden mask of her patron deity and traveled throughout the plaza to share supernatural power with her subjects. On the final day of the inauguration ceremonies a new stela was unveiled – overnight while the city slept it was erected in the plaza and wrapped in gauzy cloth. At dawn the cloth was removed and her portrait was revealed – she was shown dressed in all the official regalia of a king and standing on the back of two naked captives from a nearby polity. The lengthy hieroglyphic inscription, which she had composed herself with the help of her political advisors, described her exalted ancestors and her recent success in war (Figure 5.3).

Everyone in the city was invited to view the stela and to partake in the feasting that the royal household provided. Most of them enjoyed

---

[3] Guenter 2014.

100   *Everyday Life in the Classic Maya World*

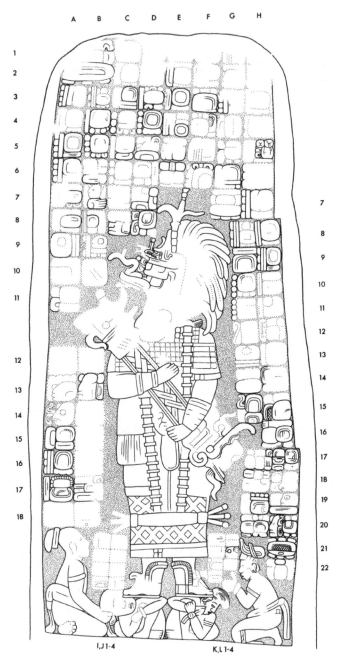

FIGURE 5.3   Portrait of Lady K'awiil Ajaw wearing Maize Deity costume and holding a ceremonial bar on stela 1 from Coba. Drawing of Coba, Stela 1, front, by Eric Von Euw with revisions by Ian Graham. © President and Fellows of Harvard College, Peabody Museum of Archaeology and Ethnology, 2004.15.6.18.1.

this part of the accession the most – they didn't need to understand how important it was that her ceremonial bar was made of the rarest of forest wood or that her jade diadems had never touched anyone else's hands and came to her directly from the king who controlled the jade sources. These festivities were what the people wanted, and she had thrown a tremendous celebration. With such an elaborate accession, no one could question the absence of a royal king. She had no brothers and was the rightful heir. Her consort could act as king when necessary, but she was the portal through which the gods of her city spoke.

Royal blood was understood to carry in it a unique form of luminous power in Classic Maya culture. For this reason, and to preserve their positions of high privilege, royal dynasties kept detailed genealogical records going back generations, sometimes into the mythical time of founding divinities. Kings and queens recounted these genealogies in hieroglyphic texts as a form of repetitive incantation. Few others outside their own royal families could read such inscriptions, but they included them over and over in official royal art. Through the recitation of the accomplishments of their ancestors, both secular and spiritual, they reinforced their own personal understanding of their unique power. Each queen was the inheritor of divine force which she passed on to only her children. For this reason many young kings paid great homage to their mothers by commissioning elaborate carved stone stelae with portraits of their mothers and texts that recounted how the king was born of such an exalted figure. New hieroglyphic decipherments indicate that royal women who had given birth to heirs acquired a special title for this accomplishment, which was certainly a defining moment in their lives and the lives of their families.[4] The need for rulers with luminous bloodlines was so great that often young royal women would be sent far from their homes to marry a young (or old) prince of a subordinate polity, in a form of diplomatic marriage alliance that tied the fate of her new home to her more powerful city of origin. Later generations would mention her arrival in the city as a defining moment in the political and spiritual life of her heirs, for in addition to bringing economic and military

---

[4] Gutierrez 2016.

support, she brought dynastic gods and powerful ancestors that she could call upon to improve the fortune of the smaller polity. Some royal women traveled hundreds of kilometers to marry into subordinate dynasties, but while a few famous kings of the Classic period are believed to have traveled great distances to found a new dynasty, none of them moved as part of a marriage alliance. This suggests the decision to marry was not in the hands of young royal women, but rather a strategic pronouncement made by the elders and advisors within her dynasty. Her children, the future rulers of allied cities, would always be spiritually connected to her family of origin, and thus likely susceptible to political and economic entanglements.

Kings and queens erected stela on special occasions in the history of their city and in the course of their lives, two narratives that were inextricably linked. The accession of a new ruler or a successful campaign of territorial expansion were both accomplishments worthy of a monument, but even more important was the commemoration of cycles of time. When one of the many cycles of time that dictated Maya lives concluded during the reign of a king or queen, the ruler had an obligation to commemorate this auspicious event. Such rituals initiated the new cycle, and thus perpetuated the movement of time and life itself. A wealthy ruler with resources to spare took great pains to observe this calendrical event correctly on behalf of their dynasty and polity. Part of performing this royal duty appropriately included the commission of a stone portrait with accompanying text that would be displayed in the semi-public areas of the city for the whole population to admire.

Another way in which royal blood was put to service was in the act of self-sacrifice. Classic Maya conceptualizations of royal blood included an understanding that blood itself, a viscous and bright substance, carried within it a type of spiritual force that was highly useful for spirit communication. Many cultures around the world and through time have acknowledged the inherent potency of human blood, both as a symbol of life force and as something greater, a manifestation of potential, a tangible reminder of the mysterious ability of human bodies to create new life. On rare and highly charged spiritual occasions, Maya royals would let their own blood, often onto bark paper, which they then would carefully burn like incense. From the smoke of this offering spirits and ancestors could appear and deliver messages or blessings. This act was so fundamental to Maya understandings of royal mediation that it is often depicted in carved stone panels that originally decorated palace walls or the detailed painted vessels that elites gave to one another as part of state visits. Queens are shown pulling a thorn-studded cord through their tongues and kings are shown drawing a barbed stingray spine through the foreskin of their penis. The scars of these activities were considered badges of honor, and the act may only have been performed once in a lifetime, but was recounted many times thereafter. The change in consciousness brought on by ritualized self-sacrifice certainly accentuated the ability of a queen or king to hear the voices of ancestors and communicate with the spirit world. Anthropologists who document the deliberate use of pain in ritualized contexts explain that the expectation and experience of pain, in a controlled setting, can cause a change in consciousness, especially when it is accompanied by other ritual acts such as chanting and prayer, rhythmic breathing, or sensory deprivation. As in other cultures, to heighten the change in consciousness, such a profound ritual sacrifice may have been accompanied by the use of entheogenic (mind-altering) substances, fasting, or prolonged physical exertion.

While we have much to learn about how Classic Maya people understood the use of entheogens, or chemical substances typically of plant origin ingested to produce a non-ordinary state of consciousness for religious or spiritual purposes, it is clear this was a component of ancient Maya religious and diplomatic life. Painted vessels depict inebriated men, surrounded by large jars (that may have held an alcoholic drink) and holding or administering enemas. Royal women are often in attendance as assistants to the most inebriated.[5] It has not yet been determined what substance was administered via enema, and while alcohol is one possibility, natural endemic hallucinogens from jimsonweed (*Datura* genus), cane toads (*Rhinella horribilis*, formerly known as *Bufo marinus*), or any of fifteen species of mushroom (*Psilocybe* genus) are all possibilities.[6] Residue from jimsonweed has been found in ceramic vessels left in caves, while toads and mushrooms are both common in Classic Maya art.[7]

[5] Seinfeld 2018.
[6] Guzman 2008.
[7] Spenard et al. 2020.

Whether through extreme physical acts such as self-sacrifice or less dramatic but equally significant acts such as bearing a healthy heir to the throne, Maya royalty spent their days in service to the members of their community and protecting their positions of privilege. Their daily needs were taken care of by servants so royals would have time for lengthy prayers, training in ritual techniques, ritualized performances on significant calendrical and dynastic occasions, and even spiritual warfare during the night. The correct and skillful performance of these sacramental responsibilities ensured successful harvests and the safety of the city. While there were undoubtedly kings and queens who were less revered than others, or who were the subject of gossip for their ritual ineptitude, one reason Maya citizens chose to live in cities was in order to be close to the royalty whom they understood to be sources of spiritual power. The economic and social prospects of urban life were plentiful, but the opportunity to witness and benefit from the spiritual mediation provided by semi-divine royalty was also clearly part of the allure of city life.

DIPLOMACY

Marriage is most often mentioned in the hieroglyphic corpus when it was the result of an alliance between polities of unequal status. The actual ceremony is rarely mentioned, and instead there is a sense that the betrothal and presentation of the bride were more commonly the topics of textual commemoration.[8] Marriages within a polity or among the non-royal members of society were hardly recorded, and we know very little about how they took place. In his 16th-century account of experiences in early colonial Yucatan, Franciscan Bishop Diego de Landa describes marriage as little more than a man moving to the home of his wife and her extended family, once the betrothal or marriage negotiations were complete. There was often a period of extended labor the new groom owed the family of his wife, and it is possible that the majority of marriages in Classic Maya society were conducted in this manner. After an expression of interest between two young people, and with the agreement of their families, food was

---

[8] Martin 2020.

prepared for the family of the groom and the couple was considered married. Divorce was just as simple, according to Bishop Landa – either party could pack up their things and leave, voiding the marriage and making themselves eligible to remarry. Subjects such as the intimate lives and personal relationships of ancient people were difficult for European chroniclers to assess accurately, and we need to read Landa with a healthy dose of skepticism. But his description of the relative simplicity of the marriage ceremony does match the almost total absence of textual or artistic evidence for marriage rituals in elite media.

However, we know more about how marriage was practiced within the ruling families of elite urban centers. This is due to the powerful role of marriage in solidifying political power, both within a dynasty and between allied polities. Throughout history, marriage has very rarely been understood to center on the personal connection of the two (or more) parties involved, and in Classic Maya elite culture, as in many other royal societies, the personal preferences of those involved were deeply subjugated to the political ambitions of their families. There are examples of marriage conducted immediately following a war of conquest, such as the marriage of the king of Naranjo, K'ahk' Tiliw Chan Chahk, to a woman of the city of Tuubal, a place his mother the queen of Naranjo had ordered burned and destroyed a few years earlier.[9] Whether this princess was captured from Tuubal, was offered to the Naranjo dynasty as a form of payment or tribute, or was chosen by the king in order to further cement his control over the royals of Tuubal, we cannot say. This is an example of the tool of marriage being used to convey political aims, including subjugation, domination, and likely the extraction of resources – a very different notion of marriage than our own today in the West, but a very customary use of marriage in the ancient world.

More commonly, the hieroglyphic record was used to commemorate the arrival of a princess from a higher-status polity. These women were often sent far from home, after negotiations between the elders of their families – arrangements that may be depicted on a limited number of elite ceramic vases. These scenes show adult men in

---

[9] Martin 2020:185.

discussion within a well-appointed palace room, as young women peak out from behind a curtain or doorway. It is likely that adult female relatives played a role in these negotiations also, as they do in arranged marriages elsewhere in the world. As discussed in the previous section on spiritual mediation, young princesses from high-status polities, such as the so-called Snake Princesses from Calakmul sent to the small but strategic site of La Corona, brought with them spiritual legitimacy as well as political connections. While their marriages may not have provided them emotional connection, there is evidence they traveled with architects and artists from their home when they moved to a lower-status city. If they had children, the bonds they shared with their offspring were likely the most stable and meaningful in their lives, again by analogy to better-documented cultures that practice marriage alliance or arranged marriage.[10] This is likely part of the reason why so many Classic Maya stelae that depict royal women were commissioned by their sons.

As marriage was understood as a powerful tool for political advancement within elite Maya culture, it should not be surprising that some Maya kings had multiple wives. The practice of polygamy has been documented in the inscriptions of multiple Classic Maya centers, as well as the resulting conflict between the progeny of these royal women who appear to have all been equally eligible to take the throne on their father's death. The best documentation of this practice comes from Yaxchilan, a site that has an extraordinary number of monuments dedicated to the accomplishments of royal women. More than one king had multiple wives in the Classic period history of Yaxchilan, but the reign of Bird Jaguar IV (752–768 CE) illustrates how complicated family life must have been within the royal palaces of polygynous kings. Bird Jaguar IV took the throne after his half-brother, Yopaat Bahlam II, disappeared. Yopaat Bahlam II was the son of a queen from Maya history who is famous for the beautiful portraits of her engaged in ritual self-sacrifice that decorated the private rooms of her palace. This woman, Ix K'abal Xook, was one of three wives of the king Shield Jaguar III, the father of both Yohpaat Bahlam II and Bird Jaguar IV. While we do not know why one of the

---

[10] Guenter and Freidel 2005.

sons was able to accede to the throne before the other, neither do we know what happened to him (was he killed by a brother in a case of royal fratricide?). Once Bird Jaguar IV was king, he removed almost all record of his half-brother's reign. This was not a sibling relationship anyone would envy, and while mother-child relationships were likely stable and nurturing, royal sibling relationships, especially between brothers, were potentially life-threatening.

The potential of brides to enhance a dynastic line with new heirs or to squander their reproductive power appears frequently in Classic Maya and Mesoamerican mythology, which are filled with many goddesses of uncontrolled sexuality that tempt the Maize Deity and others, as well as goddesses that provide rejuvenation to dying gods through their beauty and connection to the fertile earth. Control of female sexuality, especially female reproduction, was at the heart of Classic period marriage alliances. Young kings were associated with Juun Imix, the youthful maize deity who fell to his death through the temptation of sexually aggressive goddesses. The sexual nature of royal Maya women was both essential to the reproduction of dynastic lineages and fraught with the power to distract and endanger royal men. The Moon Goddess embodied this potency, and is often shown commanding mythological male figures, especially older or elderly men. Mythological scenes on painted pottery are filled with suitors disguised in the form of hummingbirds, other birds, or biting insects that distract young women who are often marked as the Moon Goddess, from their duties to old gods (perhaps her father).[11] Seduction, of both young women and young men, is ever-present and an existential risk to societies that relied on pedigrees of blood and birthright. These mythological sources provide us with a window on how tense and laden with promise, both positive and negative, marriage negotiations might have been.

Marriages were only one of the many forms of political agreement between polities of the Classic period. Royal dynasties and their associated family members and courts were the core of each political unit, or polity. These extended families, sometimes with competing branches, were centered in a particular city and its population. Thus

---

[11] Chinchilla Mazariegos 2017:87.

FIGURE 5.4 Two royal lords visiting in a palace setting on a Classic period ceramic vase. Note the bundle of sticks between them, perhaps representing a small ceremonial fire. Photo: Lowe Art Museum 89.0080.

the royalty, their physical territory, and their citizens were a self-contained political entity. However, it was advantageous for polities to band together in order to create larger political alliances and for economic reasons such as the exchange of goods and services. Such alliances were commemorated in hieroglyphic inscriptions to accompany images of state visits, which were painted on palace walls and ceramic vases. While we are far from understanding all the mechanisms of the Classic Maya economy, it appears that while each city or polity was largely self-sufficient in terms of basic necessities such as food and tools, an elaborate trading economy ran in parallel with local systems of production. Royal visits with traders are also depicted in the corpus of ceramic vases and thus we believe that elites spent much of their time visiting with foreign dignitaries from other polities and cementing such alliances through ceremonial events such as elaborate feasts and royal gifting (Figure 5.4).

The presentation of tribute to a Maya ruler was a common subject on painted vases. Kings are seated on comfortable cotton cushions that cover a low stone throne deep within the palace. Stone walls are adorned with gauzy curtains woven of white cotton draped luxuriously from ceiling to floor, softening the space so that it appeared very different from how it does to the modern visitor who sees nothing but unforgiving stone surfaces. Cotton cloth served not only to decorate the palace and create a comfortable environment for the rulers; it was one of the primary tribute items that subordinate lords and ladies brought to their ruler in order to show loyalty. Cotton grows well in the Maya area, and has been spun into thread and woven into cloth for millennia. It remains an important crop today. However in the Classic period cotton cloth was monopolized by the elite, who consumed it lavishly for furnishing rooms of the palace but also for their daily clothing, for ceremonial attire including the ball-game uniform, and for a host of ritual purposes such as wrapping stone monuments, ancestral bundles, and other precious objects. Thus the images of long bolts of hand-woven cotton cloth presented to royalty by their subjects are not just historic records of actual transactions; they are reminders to anyone who saw the painted vase of the exclusive access elites had to this all important material, and their ability to demand it from the population. Other items that were also presented as tribute within a palace diplomatic setting include baskets of cacao beans, spiny bivalve shells for jewelry, deer haunches, and copal resin incense. These objects were gifts in the sense that they were exchanges from one bureaucrat to another, but more importantly they were symbols of the patron-client relationship established through such private meetings in the palace. The presentation of baskets of precious shells to a Maya ruler was a way to materialize the relationship of protection and patronage that the subordinate expected as well as the tithing of resources on which rulers survived.

Archaeological evidence from many ancient Maya palaces shows that at some point, perhaps after trading and political negotiations were concluded, royal families hosted elaborate feasts for their visiting guests. The remains of roasted venison, turkey, and turtle have been found behind palace walls, mixed with the ceramic crockery that broke predictably during a boisterous and extended feast. Early Spanish encounters with Maya people inevitably included food that the Indigenous leaders prepared to share with their European visitors, and hospitality was taken very seriously – no guest was turned away unfed. Many pre-Columbian Maya recipes remain popular today, such as roasting seasoned venison in an underground oven known as a pib, or turkey stewed with charred peppers and eggs. These are elaborate and time-consuming dishes that require many hours of preparation and supervision, not to mention ingredients that might have been hard to obtain in the past. Perhaps some of the trade negotiations included the provisioning of the palace with rare spices or seasonings. We know that cacao, or the cocoa bean, was more plentiful in certain regions of the Maya area than others and that cacao was traded widely in addition to being gifted to the rulers in tribute. Maya people were the first to discover the wonders of chocolate and its rich, buttery texture. Cacao trees grow in humid tropical areas and were domesticated by Maya people long before chocolate was discovered by Europeans, who eventually made it into the sweet treat we know today. Classic Maya kings and queens preferred to mix ground cacao beans with chili peppers and water, pouring it from one vessel to another in order to create a thick frothy drink. The head of the resulting beverage, just like the head of a good beer, was the most desired component. Cacao and corn are the two foodstuffs mentioned most commonly in Maya inscriptions, a reflection of their dietary and social importance.[12] Cacao was depicted frequently in Maya art, in many stages of preparation: growing in pods on a tree, being ground into cacao paste on a stone metate and being mixed with liquid to create a bubbly drink. The ubiquity of cacao in Classic art, a tightly controlled media used by the elite to uphold their power, underscores the social importance of this particular plant, and the privilege associated with its consumption. Cacao drinks came in many varieties. In texts it is described as new, ripe, fermented, or sweet. It could also be flavored with honey, lima bean, cherry, or chili, and colored with the red annatto seed. In all these variations, it still contained the richness of cocoa butter, as well as the active ingredients theobromine, known as the love drug, and caffeine, both mood elevators. The ancient Maya even had their own version of chocoholics – a sculpture of a small dog from the site of Tonina is inscribed with the name of its owner, simply named as the "cacao person."[13]

As in every culture, Classic Maya people also developed alcoholic beverages by using honey as a fermentation agent. These relatively

[12] Carter and Matsumoto 2020:89.
[13] Stuart 2014.

mild meads, or honey wines, could be made fairly quickly in preparation for a feast or ceremony, but were not suitable to store for any length of time. Of course royal feasts also included many dishes made of corn, the main foodstuff of all Maya people, royal and commoner alike. Plates of tamales decorated with different elaborate salsas are depicted in elite artwork, and royal vessels are sometimes described as the queen or king's atole (corn porridge) cup from which they drank the same corn porridge as every other citizen of their polity. From isotopic analysis of skeletal material, we know that while queens may have been fortunate enough to have someone else prepare their atole, or to have a choice of spices with which to season it, they too drank and ate corn multiple times a day, just like the commoners.[14]

Queens may have supervised the preparation or even lent their hand to make some of the elaborate dishes prepared for royal feasts. Young royal women, likely princesses or attendants of the court, are depicted in art serving food and drink to visiting dignitaries. Given the elaborate nature of many Maya feast foods, one needed to be an expert in the kitchen to remember all the techniques and ingredients that consumed days of preparation. There is a close association between women and food production in contemporary Maya culture, and women are believed to be inherently better able to learn how to cook, although of course some men love to cook as well. Thus, while we lack direct evidence of how much time queens spent in preparation for a royal feast, it is quite likely the success of such events was important enough to the royal family and the prestige attached to expertly prepared food was sufficient that royal women spent time learning about Maya cuisine. The rules and rituals that guide how to prepare food and how to serve it properly in diplomatic settings are a key component of royal courts in all cultures.

Political feasts and visits may have also included entertainment for the visitors and their hosts. Royal courts kept musicians, gymnasts, and dancers who performed as part of elaborate state rituals, and these artists also may have entertained visitors in order to impress upon them the vast resources available to their hosts. Elaborately decorated dancers displayed the exotic goods their patrons controlled, and their

---

[14] Tiesler et al. 2017:95.

dances demonstrated, in an aesthetically pleasing manner, the close link between such goods and the divine basis of elite power. The dancers of royal courts were an integral part of not only how a king or queen demonstrated their wealth and economic connections, but also why subordinates needed to pay tribute and keep open the flow of exotic goods along regional trade routes. Dancers could only be trained in royal courts and their highly ideologically charged performances were viewed only by those who had access to such a venue.[15] Like the chocolate froth in the feast, or the jewels worn by the queen, royal court music and performance were courtly arts that reinforced the benefits of a patron-client relationship. A variety of drums (some the size of barrels), flutes, and bells have been found in archaeological excavations, and palace murals show that an even wider variety of musical instruments were played, including huge conch shell trumpets painted with imagery of the wind deity. In order to produce sound from a conch shell, a powerful amount of air must be blown through the shell correctly, with the result that these trumpets are always loud and dramatic instruments. A boisterous musical accompaniment to courtly feasts and dances was likely what Classic Maya rulers preferred.

COURTLY ARTS

Like fine cuisine, a variety of other refined pastimes kept the royal family busy. Many of these were more complex versions of the activities that took place in household compounds across the city. Dietary patterns are a good example of how this worked. While most people in our ancient city ate corn tamales with a few beans inside, the royalty dined on sumptuous versions of these same dishes that simultaneously signaled that they were Maya like the rest of the population (i.e., the food was corn-based) but yet different or special (their tamales were filled with rare frog eggs or seasoned with specially aged peppers). As commoner families told stories at night about the stars in the sky, the royalty memorized the movements of the planets through the constellations and wrote complex almanacs to record and predict celestial

---

[15] Looper 2009.

activity. Domestic compounds on the edges of the city likely made their own pottery for preparing and serving food, while members of the royal family painted elaborate cylinder vases with scenes of palace life. Each artwork changed the artist, and Maya ideas about art and craft were closely linked to those who performed the act of artistic creation. Men who carved wooden deity figures were linked to the fortunes of those figures for the rest of their lives. This ongoing and evolving connection to material objects was the result of the Maya view that many material items had an inherent life force, a luminosity that could bring good or ill fortune. Modern Maya shamans often ritually coerce their ritual tools such as crystals into cooperation, because they grant agency to objects, an agency close to our Western notion of personhood.[16] For the ancient Maya, certain artwork and substances such as jade or spondylus shell had power that derived from forces such as mythic beings, meteorological phenomena, or color. These powers were engaged through ritual actions, and could act on behalf of humanity or against humanity – negotiation and courtesy were required for a positive outcome. For this reason, jade was preferred over all other green stones, because it was known to have an inherent animating force that was nearly as significant as the imagery carved into the jade.

Jade was perhaps the most highly valued rare item in Classic Maya society. Much more important than gold or silver, jade jewels were essential components of royal dress, and a status marker for those who were trying to emulate elites. The significance of jade extended to other green stones, such as serpentine or even limestone painted bluish green, but it was true jade from one source in the Maya highlands of Guatemala that had the highest value (Figure 5.5). Its scarcity is believed to have contributed to its value in Maya culture – the apple green jade preferred by Maya rulers comes from tributaries within the Montagua River Valley, a single region on the southeastern periphery of the Maya world. It is found in boulders, some as large as a small car, that wash out of the mountains and into the rivers. Jade was also highly valued by earlier complex cultures of Mesoamerica, such as the Olmec, often considered the mother culture of Mesoamerica because many of the symbols of power used by Maya, Zapotec, and

---

[16] Astor-Aguilera 2020:653.

FIGURE 5.5 Portrait of a lord carved into a jade pebble. Photo: Lowe Art Museum 86.0189.

Aztec leaders such as monumental architecture, animal transformation, and jade jewels were first important to the Olmec. Jade is also extremely hard – it was the hardest material known to ancient Mesoamericans, and required extensive effort to shape into the beads, plaques, and ear flares that elites required. The investment of time required to make these objects contributed to their importance and what is described as the inalienability of their value. Inalienability refers to the ongoing and persistent connection of the craftsperson to the jade object they created, even after it was traded to another.[17] Perhaps the most dramatic reason for the importance of jade was its lustrous green color, which to Maya people resembled the shoots of a young maize plant as it broke through the earth and reached up to the sunlight. Jade encapsulated the reliance of Maya people on corn – its ability to regenerate each spring after entering the ground as a seed, its ability to mature and produce sufficient food for huge populations, and the death of the maize plant at harvest time, which in turn allowed for rebirth. The entire subsistence system of Maya society and

[17] Kovacevich 2014.

its reliance on dynastic rulership to maintain and schedule maize agriculture was epitomized by the qualities of jade.

Maya gender-specific conceptualizations about inherent abilities to work with certain materials also impacted courtly arts. Just as young women were depicted serving food and likely older women were involved in the supervision of complicated cuisine, excavations of Maya palaces often reveal an area where textile arts were practiced. Scholars agree this was likely something royal women spent time doing regularly – creating elaborate woven and embroidered cloth for royal costumes and use in ceremonial bundles. Women likely gathered, as they do today in the Maya highlands, to visit and gossip as they worked on panels of cloth. First fibers such as cotton had to be spun into fine thread using ceramic spindle weights that could be decorated with birds, flowers, and other images related to the creation of cloth. Then the thread could be dyed into a myriad of colors and eventually woven into fabric. This was an activity in which the original creator couple engaged according to Maya mythology, and cloth carried much more than just utilitarian significance. Designs drawn from complex mythology and the cycles of nature were woven into the fabric as a way to teach young members of the royal family the importance of such imagery and to reinforce the dynasty's connection to these sources of power (Figure 5.6). Each woman had her own backstrap loom, with the shuttle and other pieces made of rare hardwoods polished over time by their movement back and forth through the cotton fibers. A strap around her back allowed the weaver to lean in or away from her work to adjust the tension of the cloth, and also allowed her to see the fabric canvas on which she could embellish the background cloth with embroidery or extra woven thread. Decorative accents were added with thread made of rabbit fur, feathers, or silk floss from the ceiba tree, delicate fibers that were difficult to spin and beyond the skill level of most commoners. Other royal women preferred to create elaborate batik designs rather than embroider and used melted beeswax to paint designs on cotton cloth before it was dyed different vibrant hues of red, yellow, black, or blue.

From time to time there was a princess who had no patience for textiles or cooking and sought out her brothers and cousins in the scribal chambers. Among the company of largely young men, she would be taught how to write hieroglyphic texts and all the literary

FIGURE 5.6 Classic period ceramic figurine and rattle depicting a royal woman with elaborately woven clothing. Photo: Lowe Art Museum 85.0067.

variations that were possible in order to display one's personal style or the personality of one's patron. They practiced penmanship on clay tablets until they could write with a fluid and flowing script. Sometimes a young scribe worked out a phrase or calculation on the wall of the chamber itself. At the site of Xultun, astronomical calculations related to the movement of Mars and visible total lunar eclipses were painted and inscribed on the walls of a small room at the palace where scribes likely designed what they would later commit to bark-paper books or stone tablets.[18] The most artistically talented young

---

[18] Bricker et al. 2014.

scribes were chosen to paint texts. When they achieved a high level of skill, they were given a polished conch shell ink pot full of pigment. Using animal hair–tipped brushes with carved and decorated bone handles, which became the symbol of their art, they painted complex texts on the wet surfaces of freshly stuccoed palace walls, and on the pages of bark-paper books. Only four native Maya books survive today, and all date from the Postclassic period (1000–1450 CE), although they preserve language, cosmology, and calendrical knowledge that originated in the Classic period. These books were seen by Spanish colonial clerics as extremely dangerous implements of Indigenous pagan religion, and many hundreds were burned during the 16th century, while a handful were sent to European royalty where they eventually made their way to the national libraries of Dresden, Madrid, and Paris. The oldest of these books was found in a highland Maya cave and is known as the Maya Codex of Mexico.[19]

Pigments of black, red, yellow, and even blue-green minerals were produced on small stone mortars and kept in the rooms where scribes worked in order to make small batches of ink as needed. Palace walls and floors were covered in only the finest plaster, made by experts who had access to the best limestone sources and knew exactly how long to burn rock in order to create a fine powder that was uniformly white and even. Those scribes who were more interested in mythology than in the calendar or writing might be trained to decorate palace walls with scenes of cosmological significance to the royal family, or perhaps to record an especially influential royal visit. A particularly important example of Maya muralism is found at the Late Preclassic site of San Bartolo, where beautifully preserved murals adorned the interior walls of a small ritual room. These calligraphic renderings of humans, animals, and landscapes were painted in vibrant colors and have short accompanying texts. The subject matter is cosmological – a narrative story unfolds to tell the story of the birth, death, and rebirth of the Maize Deity and his avatar on earth, a recently enthroned king. Scholars think this temple room was a private area, where a small number of elites performed divination or bloodletting rituals. The complexity of the imagery would likely not have been understood by

---

[19] Coe et al. 2015.

most of the population, who had limited access to such iconography.[20] The accession of a new ruler was always an occasion for the replastering of older walls that could then be decorated with either texts or imagery; some rulers took an intense interest in texts, learning to write passages themselves. In a quiet moment when scribes were not working on something commissioned by their patron, they might scratch into the plaster wall a caricature of the king during one of his pompous ceremonies. Graffiti is common in Maya palaces and not all of it was made by those who had artistic skill – sometimes it seems as if bored attendants or children took the opportunity to entertain themselves with stick figures and fantastic beasts (Figure 5.7).

Some royal scribes worked with stonemasons to create texts that would accompany images of their patrons on stelae and stone lintels. Phrases were worked out well in advance as carvers had to work quickly while the limestone panel remained soft enough to carve after it was quarried. Mistakes were sometimes made and a less practiced scribe might demonstrate their inexperience by carving the text in glyphic blocks of unequal size. The prestige of being a scribe was higher than any other – they were the only artists in Classic Maya culture who were allowed to sign their personal names to their work. Given the complexity of the writing system and how rarely we find hieroglyphic inscriptions outside elite contexts, it is unlikely that anyone not of royal descent was permitted to learn the textual arts. By allowing only those from royal families to write, Maya rulers conserved the power provided by the ability to record history. When only those in power are able to record and thus create historical records, power is conserved within that same social group. In Classic Maya times, history was not an impartial recounting of events; it was a tool wielded by the elite against one another in order to compete for and maintain power.

Maintaining control of the reckoning of time was an important component of how Classic Maya rulers controlled the historical record and their central role in the administration of the city. Stelae almost always record dates in reference to the multiple cycles of time within

---

[20] Hurst 2020:585.

Palace Life

FIGURE 5.7 Example of graffiti carved in the stucco of a palace wall, Tikal, Guatemala. Image courtesy of the Penn Museum, Figure 10a. *The Graffiti of Tikal*, Tikal Report 31 (1983). Graffiti on east wall of room 2, structure 3d-40, Tikal.

the Maya calendar, and bark-paper codices were full of accurate astronomical predictions. From these data as well as the alignments of major architecture and the rare painted calculations on palace walls, we know royal Maya families included skilled astronomers and mathematicians. This allowed them to choose auspicious dates for all major events such as marriages, accessions, the sealing of an alliance, or the initiation of war. Perhaps even more important, it allowed ruling families to create written records that manipulated the timing of historical events to coincide with significant astronomical or calendrical phenomena. The many cycles of the Maya calendar, which record not only the solar year but much longer periods of time, derive from a cosmological belief in the multiple creations (and destructions) of the world. Keeping track of these cycles required sophisticated training in literacy, mathematics, and observational astronomy. Royal palace scribes are known to have recorded the cycles of lunar months, patterns of lunar and solar eclipses, the 584-day-long synodic period of Venus (the time Venus takes to be seen in the same position in the sky), the 117-day-long synodic period of Mercury, and the 780-day-long period of Mars, and some scholars believe there is evidence they tracked and recorded the movements of Jupiter as well.[21] The planets were understood to be a guide into the harmonious and predictable workings of the universe, and thus timing key rituals or activities of the royal court to planetary movements preserved the appearance of order and the continuation of royal life.

Maya urban centers grew in haphazard ways, dictated it seems by the whims and desires of those rulers who controlled sufficient resources to mount building campaigns. But underlying these expansions were overarching ideas about space, including the importance of directional alignments that followed the points of the compass. Many Maya sites are aligned on an axis that is just east of north-south, although major palace and temple acropoli are situated in all points of the compass. One ritual architectural complex appears at scores of Maya sites across the lowlands, and it has come to be known as an E Group. Characterized by a pyramid, often equal sided, on the western side of a plaza or open area that is bounded by a long structure on the eastern side, E Groups were the earliest monumental architecture built in a repeated fashion at multiple sites. What is even more fascinating about these complexes is that in their earliest forms, during the Preclassic period, they are astronomical observatories. To

---

[21] Bricker and Bricker 2011.

someone standing on the western pyramid structure, the sun would rise over the doorways in the eastern structure on the solstices and equinoxes. Astronomy may have been a shared practice that linked Maya people across vast areas of the lowlands and helped integrate new settlements of proto-agriculturalists. Excavation of these groups shows that the ground where they were built was prepared elaborately prior to construction, and even the bedrock was occasionally carved with symbols. Caches of special objects were deposited in the floors and buildings as they were built, and ritual artifacts were left in the structures.[22] The movements of the sun were likely linked to ideas about time keeping, renewal, and celebrations. Later in the Classic period, older E Group buildings were modified into even more elaborate structures, and the astronomical emphasis shifted to the solar zenith passage, or the day when the sun passes directly overhead. This often fell near the equinoxes at the latitude of most Maya centers, but archaeoastronomer Anthony Aveni suggests it was tied more closely to the dynastic control of planting and harvest than to the sun.[23] Throughout time and at many different Maya cities, E Groups provided an architectural space tied to the calendar that aided the scheduling of agriculture, marketing, and dynastic control of food production. These plazas and structures also provided stages for elites to perform dramatic rituals tied to the movement of the planets and constellations, thus demonstrating esoteric knowledge possessed by very few people within Classic society. In this way they drew commoners and elites together and helped cement the fragile ties between rulers and ruled.

Members of the royal family also learned how to craft jade pebbles into elaborate portraits of the Maize Deity, how to work shell or pyrite into mosaic mirrors and jewelry, and how to paint cylindrical ceramic vases that commemorated significant events in the life of the royal court. All of these art forms were tightly controlled by their occurrence within the palace walls as well as their attachment to the members of the royal family. In contrast to many other ancient states, there does not appear to have been a class of non-royal artistic specialists who lived in compounds where they produced art to fill

---

[22] Chase et al. 2017.
[23] Aveni and Dowd 2017.

the warehouses of the king. In Classic Maya society, most if not all complex art was produced, or at least the finishing touches were applied, within palace compounds by specialists who had direct ties to the royal family or were members of the ruling dynasty. This greatly facilitated the control of iconographic messaging so that kings and queens were the only ones who could commission major works of art, leaving them almost entirely in control of the artistic record of their cities.

The small percentage of ancient Maya people who lived within palace compounds are responsible for a vast array of the data we use to understand this ancient culture. These walled enclosures of small, dark rooms around private courtyards were filled with many members of the extended royal family as well as their attendants. Vulnerable to the rare incursions of foreign raiders and the more common machinations of competing dynasties, royals likely circulated within a relatively small social circle of family members and trusted servants. State visits were a welcome opportunity to socialize with peers who shared an appreciation for the courtly arts of debate, feasting, and performance. These visits also presented a chance to display the fine art created within the palace by scribes, stone carvers, and painters the king supported. Discussion of calendrical omens might have concluded with stargazing and the display of bark-paper almanacs. In quieter moments, the palace royalty worried about the fortunes of their polities and prayed for the benevolence of their dynastic gods. Although palace life represents only a small fraction of the ancient Maya experience, the belief that royalty descended from deities and carried within their blood a semi-divine nature, coupled with social structures that kept the commoner population subject to such beliefs, provided elite palace culture with a defining role in Classic Maya culture.

Suggested Readings

Aveni, Anthony 2001 *Skywatchers of Ancient Mexico*. Austin: University of Texas Press.
Coe, Michael D., and Justin Kerr 1998 *The Art of the Maya Scribe*. New York: Harry N. Abrams.
Freidel, David A., Arlen F. Chase, Anne S. Dowd, and Jerry Murdock, eds. 2017 *Maya E Groups: Calendars, Astronomy, and Urbanism in the Early Lowlands*. Gainesville: University Press of Florida.

Guenter, Stanley 2014 The Queen of Coba: A Reanalysis of the Macanxoc Stelae. In *The Archaeology of Yucatan*, ed. T. Stanton, pp. 395–421. Oxford: Archaeopress.

Hendon, Julia A. 1997 Women's Work, Women's Space and Women's Status among the Classic Period Maya Elite of the Copan Valley, Honduras. In *Women in Prehistory*, ed. C. Claassen and R. A. Joyce, pp. 33–46. Philadelphia: University of Pennsylvania Press.

Looper, Matthew G. 2009 *To Be Like Gods: Dance in Ancient Maya Civilization*. Austin: University of Texas Press.

Miller, Mary, and Simon Martin 2004 *Courtly Art of the Ancient Maya*. San Francisco, CA: Fine Arts Museum of San Francisco.

6

To the Coast

While most discussions of Maya culture emphasize the central importance of maize agriculture to Maya identity and daily life, interregional trade in natural resources from a huge variety of micro-environments was equally central to the everyday habits of Maya people during the Classic period. The Yucatan peninsula makes up the majority of the landmass where Maya-speaking people lived in the past, and it is defined by an enormous coastline with hundreds of barrier islands and shallow bays. At the base of the peninsula there are river systems that flow from the southern Maya lowlands out to the Gulf of Mexico and the Caribbean Sea. Goods from the highlands and southern lowlands moved along these rivers, and then in turn up the coastline. Inland farmers, craftspeople, and their rulers relied on coastal trade for daily necessities, not just exotic jewelry and ritual items. Traders frequented coastal settlements, which were some of the most diverse and interesting places in the Classic period, where people from throughout the Maya world and beyond met and exchanged ideas as well as goods. These ports of trade emphasized economic exchange over dynastic lineage as a means to acquire influence and power, although some ports were controlled by large inland dynastic cities and certain commodities seem to have moved in and out of trade centers based on political alliances crafted or destroyed by the elite. The daily activities of those who lived near the sea were different from those of Maya people who lived at inland centers, and full- and part-time traders held positions of great influence in Maya society. In addition to economic activity, coastal settlements were often places of spiritual significance, even pilgrimage, as they embodied Maya conceptualizations of the sea as a boundary place between one world and another. Scenes from Classic mythology show supernatural creatures traveling to the underworld on a carved wooden canoe – and perhaps in part for its ability to provide not only subsistence but also rare materials, the sea was understood as a metaphor for the primordial place of origin, a realm where deities and potent spirits resided (Figure 6.1).

TRAVELING TO THE SEA

Coastal settlements were filled with people from rural and urban households who found themselves wanting a different life, perhaps one they saw as providing more economic opportunity or more diverse social interactions.[1] A young person from the rural domestic compound we discussed in Chapter 2 might have left their family of origin to live on the coast, learning the skills of fishing and how to be a useful crew member on a large trading canoe. Perhaps Chel, or Rainbow, lived with an extended family member who made the same choice to move to the coast generations ago, and now owned multiple fishing canoes used to provide seafood for the family, harvesting extra for trade. Their day would start early, before dawn, when they rose to eat the same corn porridge they ate when they lived near the cornfields of their former inland home. On the coast it was harder to find as many different kinds of fruit to add to a morning breakfast, so instead they had salted and spiced fish, which left them full and ready for work. Just as the sun was rising, Chel left with relatives on a daily fishing expedition, with nets and spears. The family would look for the easy fish in shallow waters today, since it was stormy, and perhaps catch a duck there too. By midday they would be out of the strong sun and back at home, processing their catch, repairing nets, and sharing stories about the newest trader to arrive in their town. Chel had always felt confined by the gendered expectations of domestic chores or tending the cornfields, and enjoyed the freedom of a coastal life.

[1] Tiesler et al. 2005.

FIGURE 6.1 Rollout photograph of the Star Wars Vase, showing twin Maize Deities in a wooden canoe. University of Miami Special Collections, Jay I. Kislak Collection. Photo: Marc Zender and Simon Martin.

The coastal settlement was a two-day walk from the city of Coba. Some ports were closer to their capitals, but most large cities were located well inland in order to take advantage of natural resources and the inherent defensive advantages of higher ground. As one left the city, the landscape changed gradually, and by the second day of walking, the ground was wetter, but stone walkways that facilitated official movement between the city and the coast during the rainy time of the year had been built to make the journey quicker. The trees and animals were different in this region as well, with many rare and valuable resources controlled by the urban polity. Tropical savannah wetlands were filled with hardwoods for carving into canoes and palace lintels, a variety of palms used for thatching all the homes of the city as

To the Coast

FIGURE 6.1 (*cont.*)

well as for making the fine palm fiber cloth used by royalty to cover palace floors, and a host of other medically or economically useful plants. White mangrove leaves were used to make an astringent for the skin or a tonic to prevent dysentery, while chicle trees provided a sap that could be chewed to stave off hunger and clean teeth (chicle later became the basis for modern chewing gum). Jaguars, one of the preeminent Maya symbols of the power of the natural world and thus an important avatar of many kings and queens, loved the inaccessible savannah wetlands and especially the abundant peccary, deer, and other wildlife that lived there too. The stone walkway through the wetlands passed freshwater wells and tree islands, natural areas of higher ground in this perennially wet environment, where animals gathered and a traveler could replenish drinking water or rest on mostly dry ground. Eventually, the ground sloped even closer to the sea and travelers entered the mangrove forest that hugs the coast of the

Yucatan peninsula. Natural passages formed by freshwater currents that flowed through the tangled mangrove were enlarged into canals by boatmen who would transport travelers and goods by canoe to the coast. During this part of the journey the animal life changed once again, as the mangrove was home to water birds, alligators, crocodiles, raccoons, and manatees. Within an hour of launching the boat, the smell of salt water signaled the journey was nearly complete.

Along the Caribbean coast there are many sites that might have served as the port for Coba, the ancient city that inspired this book. The most convincing candidate is Muyil, due to its architectural and artifactual similarities to the huge urban city of the interior.[2] Most of the sites along the Caribbean coast flourished hundreds of years after the Classic period, during the Late Postclassic period (1200–1450 CE) when Maya traders interacted with the emerging states of central Mexico, including the Aztec Empire. These later sites, such as Tulum or Xcaret, are well known to tourists who visit the Caribbean area today. But there are also coastal sites that date to the Classic period and even earlier, showing that coastal occupation was always important to Maya culture. These sites look much like inland cities. They have a central administrative and ceremonial core surrounded by elite living structures and a supporting population. Often the architects and masons at these sites used shell and sand to fill the platforms they built, rather than the limestone and soil more common inland, but the designs and construction techniques were largely the same. Stelae with images of rulers and hieroglyphic texts were erected in plazas, and aqueducts carried water through the central settlement. Muyil has a large pyramid in the style of those built at Coba during the Classic period, with a steep face that made climbing the steps to the temple at the top a task that required skill and dexterity (Figure 6.2). Just like at larger centers, these summit temples were probably used for ceremonial occasions, and the elite of coastal settlements may have been carried to the top of the pyramid, dressed in exotic finery visible to the population below. Or perhaps the rulers of Coba made the journey to the coast on occasion, to bless the population that provided them with a secure flow of goods from other Maya regions and from

[2] Witschey 1988.

FIGURE 6.2 Muyil Structure 1, the tallest pyramid on site with close similarities to Nohoch Mul pyramid at nearby Coba. Photo: Walter R. T. Witschey.

the sea. This pyramid is tall enough that from its summit anyone approaching the site via water would have been visible for hours in advance of their arrival, and thus this temple may have also served as a watchtower.

The main architectural groups of coastal sites are often connected by raised roads, and at Muyil, a series of Maya roads runs from the site through the wetlands and coastal mangrove forest to the water's edge. This site, like many others in the Maya world, is an inland seaport, located on a freshwater lagoon that in turn connects to the sea (Figure 6.3). The lagoon system provided additional security, in terms of both limiting access to the site and the rich natural resources available in this shallow body of calm water. Along the coast, freshwater springs feed these lagoons, which were rich in water birds, turtles, and muddy water fish. Lagoons also provided a natural harbor

FIGURE 6.3 The Caribbean coast at Muyil. A canal joins the Muyil Lagoon with the Chunyaxche Lagoon, which in turn joins the Caribbean Sea. Photograph by the author.

for traders and others moving over the water who traveled in large wooden canoes powered by a crew of oarsmen. Although these canoes are reported by 16th century Spaniards to have held as many as fifty men, they were not stable enough for long-distance, open-water travel. Like other New World Indigenous people, Maya sailors made canoes from a single huge hardwood tree that was felled, dried, and then processed with a smoldering fire built along its length. Coastal lagoons, bays, and inlets provided the perfect location for a port of trade given the maritime technology available in the Classic period.

Islands were also popular places for ancient Maya settlement. Usually located less than a mile from the coast, over a hundred barrier islands were occupied in the past, often for hundreds of years. The Yalahau Lagoon region on the northeastern coast of the Yucatan peninsula has a handful of sites that were occupied continuously from the Middle Preclassic period (700–200 BCE) through the Late Postclassic period (1200–1521 CE) by people who seem to have shared a relatively consistent cultural identity during those two millennia.[3] From the large number of burials recovered on some of these islands and the dense architecture, we know that significant numbers of people called them home. Island residents, like their coastal neighbors, relied on a mix of inland and marine resources, and even small island settlements have evidence that people ate plenty of corn and venison that likely originated on the mainland. Classic Maya ideology used the metaphors of a turtle floating in water or a mountain surrounded by the sea to describe the location of the earth within the cosmos. In this sense island settlements took on additional cosmological significance, and often had many temples or altars where people could celebrate the unique nature of island life. Elite Maya art makes clear that canoe travel over the sea was an allegory for the transition from life to death, the movement from the world of the living to the underworld of spirits and ancestors. These ideas drew many people to visit island settlements for spiritual rather than economic reasons. Traders and others who moved commodities over the sea may have been understood to travel with a divine sanction or justification, similar to those who made the journey to visit an island temple and leave a clay figurine offering.

Our young fisher person, on their trip into the lagoon, likely had access to a stone dock where boats could be secured, and at some coastal sites there are piers leading from the water's edge to facilitate boat launching. As sea levels have risen over the past 1,000 years since the Classic period, some of the features visible to ancient fisherfolk are now submerged, but sea walls, bridges, piers, and docks have all been documented at coastal Maya sites.[4] At the largest sites, facilities were built to accommodate hundreds of canoes at a time. Residents of coastal settlements spent time planning how to enhance natural features of the landscape, such as an opening in the outer sand banks or a break in the coral reef. Widening or maintaining these natural features was done alongside the construction of new structures such as docks or sea walls. A 330-meter-long seawall is one of the most dramatic features of the island site known as Isla Cerritos, first occupied in the Late Formative period. Scholars think this wall, built 80 meters off the southern side of the island, created a calm water

---

[3] Glover 2012.
[4] Andrews 2008.

harbor for canoe traders and fisherfolk.[5] The seawall has two or possibly three entrances, and at the main one in the center of the wall there are small platforms on either side of the entrance that might have supported perishable guardhouses or tollhouses where the island may have taxed long-distance traders. All around the island evidence survives of docks and piers that would have provided a small marina with landings and berths for sailors. Improvements to the coastal landscape made these settlements safer and more conducive to trade, but also required a significant amount of work to hold off the constant efforts of the ocean to wear down and wash away such waterscape alterations and constructions.

COASTAL ACTIVITIES

Like fisherfolk around the world, Classic Maya fishers went out in the early morning, when the water was calm. By mid-morning they would return with a canoe full of fish, shellfish, fowl, and marine animals. Although we do not fully understand the degree to which some coastal residents may have been full-time fishers focused on supplying dried fish for trade, isotopic analysis of inland populations shows very little marine protein was consumed at most sites away from the coast.[6] If fish was prepared for trade, this was likely done by part-time fishers who were also in search of food for their own families. What extra they were able to harvest was exchanged for corn, beans, honey, and other products that were not as easy to generate near the sea. Fishing technology was extensive in the Classic period, including different bone hooks, stone spear points, traps, and especially nets (Figure 6.4). Rich coastal lagoons were filled with small, easily netted fish, and the remains of catfish and snook are common in coastal trash heaps, or what archaeologists call middens. Fishers also gathered large amounts of shellfish, especially on the western and northern parts of the peninsula that extend into the waters of the Gulf of Mexico. Conch, oyster, and scallop shells are all common in the construction fill of coastal sites, and additional shellfish were gathered not for food but for use in ornament production. Repetitive activity skeletal

---

[5] Andrews et al. 1988.
[6] Mansell et al. 2006.

FIGURE 6.4 Stela depicting a Classic Maya fisherman with a string of fresh fish. The stela was likely moved to the church of Santa Barbara, where it is found today, from a site along the western coast of the Yucatan peninsula such as Chunchucmil. Illustration by Travis Stanton.

markers left on the bones of fishers who lived at the important coastal port of Xcambo show that highly efficient nets and traps were the most common means of catching fish, up to and including sharks who asphyxiate quickly if caught in a net or fish trap.[7] According to the ways these repetitive activities impacted their skeletons, these same people also used a bow and arrow from their canoes to shoot larger fish, and spears to wound sharks or sea turtles.

Sea turtles and ducks are the most common faunal remains found at coastal sites in the Maya area, and likely all coastal residents knew how to predict the season sea turtles would come ashore to lay eggs and make themselves available for easy capture. In addition to rich, delicious meat, popular as well with later Europeans who traveled the Caribbean, sea turtle eggs are an important source of protein, and sea turtle carapace is a super durable material from which flexible tools and ornaments were made. Very large chert and obsidian knives are found at coastal sites that were likely used for butchering sea turtle or manatee, many of which weighed hundreds or even thousands of pounds. Unlike most other wild game, once captured sea turtles can be kept alive for months and represent an important a type of food storage that is rarely available in the tropics. Freshwater turtle from the lagoons and rivers that emptied into the sea was also a popular meal at coastal sites. Shark, manta ray, and large deep-sea fish like grouper were filleted, washed in the sea, salted, and left to dry in the sun or smoked over wood fires. This helped preserve the meat so it could be stored or traded to inland sites. At the salt-producing site of Paynes Creek, in Belize, large chert knives used to gut and fillet fish were found alongside the tools used to make salt cakes, suggesting that both salted fish and salt cakes were commodities traded out from this coastal site.[8] Large ceramic jars made for carrying water with the use of a tumpline – or strap around the forehead that distributes the weight of a pack to the spine rather than the shoulders – could have been filled with conch in sea water and carried inland as well.

Maya boats were almost uniformly large wooden dugout canoes, common throughout the Caribbean, Florida, and other nearby coastal areas. Coastal residents would send a party inland to search for large

---

[7] Götz 2012.
[8] McKillop and Aoyama 2018.

cedar or dogwood trees to cut down and float to the coast via canals or rivers. These large trees were left to season and dry, then a small smoldering fire was built along the length of the tree. Once carbonized, this wood could be easily carved out with stone axes or conch shell scrapers, and gradually the interior of the canoe was formed. A slow process that benefited from many hands, the result was a long-lasting, water-tight vessel with a high center of gravity but ample cargo space. Images from Maya art show that these boats had low side walls with a flattened bow and stern not much higher than the interior space. Paddles were carved from the same wood and had a wide blade to help move the craft through the water. An original Late Classic wooden paddle was discovered in 2004, buried in sediment and mangrove peat where a lack of oxygen preserved the wooden organic elements.[9] It looked remarkably like the paddles depicted in Classic Maya art, and those used today. After conservation, a 3D scan was made of this 1,300-year-old paddle, and both are now on display at a museum in Punta Gorda, Belize.

The care and upkeep of vessels and fishing technology likely consumed a large part of the days of Classic Maya fishers, just as it does of all people who try to battle the erosive effects of salt water on wood, fiber, and stone. Fishing nets and traps were woven of plant fibers carefully selected to withstand salt water for as long as possible, but likely needed daily maintenance. Stone weights of equal size and heft are often found at coastal sites and remind us that durable stone from the Maya highlands was also necessary for fishing. Baskets for collecting shellfish and fish were made of plant fibers found in the wetlands, and needed regular replacement. Hooks, gigs, and fishing net shuttles were all made of bone that had to be carved and, since they were easily lost, replaced often. These were activities that could be done with friends and family, in the shade of a palm tree and after the hard work of fishing and hunting was complete. In these conversations, coastal people might have shared what they had seen on the water that day, a large school of manta ray, a shark that got away, a sign that the weather would change. Sharing information about life on the water was necessary for everyone's survival in this uniquely precarious

---

[9] McKillop et al. 2014.

environment, but it also created bonds and ideas about how the rhythm of life should unfold. While Classic Maya art rarely portrays those who spent their lives near the sea, from Spanish descriptions of canoe expeditions and skeletal activity markers, it is clear that men were understood to have an inherent ability to fish and power large wooden canoes. Certainly, not only men were involved in harvesting the rich resources available to coastal populations, but in Classic Maya culture, as in many Indigenous New World societies, daily activities defined one's identity, including one's gender. The provisioning of raw resources for a family, whether the substance was octopus or corn, which were in turn transformed into a meal by female relatives, was a key component of what it meant to be male. Teaching young boys to fish reinforced the expectation that they would be excellent fishermen, and sharing stories at the end of a day on the water was a way Maya men circulated a shared expectation of what it meant to be a man.

Coastal populations also facilitated the travel of pilgrims en route to island shrines. The most famous ancient Maya island with a rich history of pilgrimage is Cozumel, but other islands were also important ritual centers with an abundance of shrines. Few of these features have been investigated by archaeologists, but on Cozumel there is a network of small shrines built over freshwater wells (cenotes) and caves. Pools of fresh water that spring from underground and are accessible within the large chamber of a cave were the most common places for offerings. Jade jewelry, human bone, and marine shell were left in these sorts of caves on Cozumel, along with hundreds of small ceramic figurines. Sixteenth-century Spanish accounts record that hundreds of Maya people made the journey to Cozumel to make offerings to a deity that protected women in childbirth and brought them healing. The channel between the mainland and Cozumel is a difficult one to traverse due to a strong current, so the journey, like many pilgrimage experiences at sites all over the world, could have been a dangerous one. As discussed in earlier chapters, caves were important ritual locations at inland ancient Maya cities as well as on islands, and we still do not understand the full significance of islands as places where ancient Maya people went to petition their gods. Perhaps the journey was a reenactment of the journey into life, given how canoe travel was often used as a metaphor for the journey after death. The many stone temples and deity figures on the islands of the Maya area await further study and explanation.

TRADERS AND THEIR GOODS

Being born into a family of traders was one of the clearest means by which a non-royal person could ascend to a position of influence and relative prosperity in Classic Maya times. While we do not know what percentage of the population could be described as full-time traders, it is likely many people engaged in part-time trade in surplus goods they made at home. Evidence also suggests down-the-line trade, where surplus nonlocal materials were passed on to neighbors in exchange for something else of use. But the widespread extent of trade within the Classic Maya world argues for the additional presence of specialists in the movement of goods across long distances, professional traders who traveled by canoe or over land and knew the routes and transport conditions between large polities. Spanish colonial sources report that traders had to pay tribute to the rulers in whose realms they lived and traded, and it is likely that a system like this existed earlier in the Classic period as well. Within the Classic Maya hieroglyphic corpus, no one takes the title of merchant as later colonial period Maya leaders were known to do, but there is a term, ebeet, that seems to be attached to important individuals who traveled between royal courts. These individuals are depicted in a standard costume that include a long white cotton mantle and a bright orange spondylus shell necklace, both important long-distance trade items.[10] Ebeet seem to be tasked with conveying messages and gifts between rulers – they do not appear in the depictions of royal court functions nor do their members seem to include royals. It is very tempting to see connections between the ebeet and later Aztec pochteca, professional merchants who acted as spies gathering intelligence for the Aztec Empire as they moved precious goods throughout the realm.

Painted ceramic vases owned by elites show merchants as colorful characters making presentations of their goods in royal courts from time to time, suggesting that traders were attached to dynastic rulers

---

[10] Tokovinine and Beliaev 2013:178.

in some manner. Distinctive by their non-Maya facial characteristics, they are sometimes darker skinned from their time outside palace compounds walking in the sun, and often carry items on their backs or lay them down on the palace floor in front of kings and queens. "He of the canoe" is a title that appears with a few high-status individuals in the hieroglyphic record, including a royal family member from the site of Bonampak and its dependents, but it is likely this title is associated with military activity rather than just trade. However, it is quite likely that trade relations between polities were altered by the shifting alliances and aggressions that characterized the Classic period. There are also a few images of processions of men dressed in loincloths, carrying walking sticks that may have doubled as weapons, and wearing tumplines. Merchants used tumplines to transport goods such as ceramics, cotton cloth, and perishables. These individuals were likely merchants engaged in economic activity rather than religious processions, but it is possible that trade carried religious or spiritual connotations that should not be overlooked.

There is a god of traders, known as God L or possibly Itzam Aat (creator snail[11]), who is depicted much as we expect a full-time Maya trader to appear – older, male, tanned, muscular, and strong enough to carry a large wooden back rack (a frame larger than a backpack) full of pottery, obsidian that originated in the mountains, or other necessary goods. His name references the creator deity Itzamna and the power of the earth, which indicates both the fundamental importance Maya people placed on trade and exchange, as well as their acknowledgment of the bounty of important products that originate in the natural world. God L wears a distinctive woven palm frond sombrero to shield himself from the sun and is deliberately depicted with a non-Maya facial appearance (Figure 6.5). His Roman nose and protruding chin identify him as an outsider and physically unattractive by Classic Maya standards of beauty, although he shares jaguar ears with the Jaguar God of the Underworld, another important deity in Maya mythology. His source of wealth is a supernatural cacao tree that grows in the underworld. Perhaps Itzam Aat protects his merchant travelers with the heightened senses of a jaguar, so they will never be

---

[11] Tokovinine and Beliaev 2013:186.

To the Coast

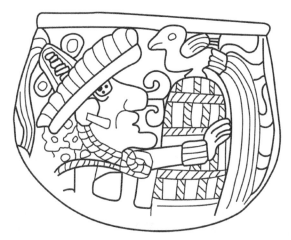

FIGURE 6.5 God L depicted on a carved ceramic vessel from Chunchucmil, Mexico. Illustration by the author and Justin Lowry.

ambushed while in transit. God L is also often shown smoking a cigar, which in addition to being a reflection of the access traders had to specific goods like tobacco, ties him to an important event in the lives of the Hero Twins during their defeat of the Lords of the Underworld (another example of the importance of journeys and travelers in Maya belief). What God L lacks in appearance he more than makes up for in exotic goods, supernatural powers of protection, and exciting stories. Maya mythology and art include depictions of the defeat and humiliation of God L, which scholars have interpreted as a reflection of the need to ensure that royal dynastic power remained the primary source of power in the Classic period, and to keep the wealth of traveling merchants both in check and tied closely to the palace.

Skeletal analysis of port-of-trade internments shows that traders did appear somewhat different from most of the population at inland Maya cities. A higher percentage of people at coastal sites have unusual head shaping or tooth filing, both aesthetic body modifications with regional patterns. Since head shaping takes place in infancy, the family of origin for someone with an unusual cranial treatment was easily identifiable as nonlocal (Figure 6.6). Long days paddling canoes and walking extended distances carrying heavy loads left many traders more muscular and with broader shoulders than urban-dwelling Maya people, and perhaps with darker skin, other

FIGURE 6.6 Rollout photograph of a Classic Maya vase depicting traders presenting folded cotton to a lord in his palace, K5453. The bundle in front of the lord may indicate the quantity of goods. Photo: Justin Kerr, K5453, Dumbarton Oaks, Trustees for Harvard University, Washington, DC.

visible signals of difference. Materials were traded across the entire Maya area, from the Pacific coast of Guatemala to northern Yucatan, and from Veracruz to Belize. At certain points in history, trade connections extended beyond this region into the Basin of Mexico and Central America. In order to move through this complex cultural and environmental landscape, negotiating the best deals, it was advantageous for a trader to know many languages and cultural traditions. Traders not only looked slightly different from most of the people with whom they interacted; they also spoke differently, ate unusual foods, and understood the customs of many diverse peoples.

Two of the most ubiquitous trade items found throughout the Maya area are both minerals from the highlands of Guatemala. Basalt for making durable grinding stones to process dried corn into flour and obsidian for all manner of cutting tools are found in almost every Maya household and palace throughout the Classic period. For this reason they are considered commodities, necessary for daily use. And the sheer amount of these materials that moved from the highlands into the lowlands is staggering. The Classic Maya did not have any domesticated pack animals, so all goods moved on the backs of human travelers who created inventive racks, nets, and frames for carrying large quantities of goods using the strength of their backs, neck, and shoulders. Basalt, a dense and durable rock formed in lava flows after a volcanic eruption, was plentiful only in the mountains of the Maya highlands. Much of the Maya world lacked stone hard enough to crush dried corn without crumbling into gritty flour. Thus basalt and its relative, granite, were both important commodities needed by every household, and a well-worn grinding stone was likely a cherished heirloom. Obsidian, a glass formed during volcanic activity in the Maya highlands, was carried by traders in large standardized chunks, roughened on the outside and wrapped in plant fibers to prevent the volcanic glass from cutting into the hands of a trader or his client. These chunks, or cores, were then traded to people who knew how to strike long, consistent blades from the core until it was worn down into a tiny bit of glass that would no longer provide new tools and could be discarded. Distance from the obsidian source contributed to how easy it was to obtain sufficient cores and blades but so did the political alliances of a polity or region. For example, Coba has an abundance of obsidian from the Classic period, while nearby large sites have very little, despite all of them being thousands of kilometers from the highlands. Did the rulers of Coba have an agreement with full-time traders who moved obsidian out of the mountains and into the rest of the Maya area? Or were the rulers of intermediary polities interested in benefiting from trade with the large, populous city? The precise mechanisms of the ancient Maya economy are still elusive to us. Traders moving out of the highlands to the Maya lowlands with basalt or obsidian likely also knew where to obtain jade, another highland resource in demand at all royal centers, but it is less likely they knew how to obtain salt or cacao, two other important trade items that were moved across the Maya area but that originated in other regions.

Salt was plentiful on the northern and western coasts of Yucatan, primarily at two major natural salt pans where salt crystals can be raked up from the ground surface. It could also be produced by boiling sea water or other brine into a residue to form salt cakes, which is a much more labor- and time-intensive process that became necessary in the Classic period due to an enormous need for salt. Brine boiling has been documented in both coastal Belize and the Pacific coast of Guatemala, where people were far from the northern lowland salt pans and possibly excluded from the political alliances that made this north coast salt available to inland cities. It is hard for us to imagine how important the salt trade was in Classic times, given our easy access to this natural resource today, but in hot climates especially, salt acts to replace electrolytes lost during physical exertion, and low sodium levels can aggravate dehydration. The addition of salt to food was a biological necessity for most inland Maya people, who ate a diet of primarily plant foods low in natural sodium and very little meat. In addition to human dietary needs, salt was used to preserve food, treat medical conditions, stiffen fabric for protective purposes, offer to the gods, and a host of other purposes. Salt traders were important enough to appear in the market murals at Calakmul, where a vendor is shown selling salt by the spoonful from a basket and is labeled with a hieroglyphic caption that reads, "he or she of salt."

Cacao was found most abundantly in the river valleys of the southern lowlands, especially in Belize. People grew cacao in other parts of the Maya world, especially in soil-rich sinkholes of the northern lowlands, but cacao is a delicate plant that requires specific moisture and tending. Traders from Belize likely carried large cloth bags of dried cacao beans to the river, and then traveled by boat through the bays and inlets of the Caribbean coast to trade their cacao beans for other precious goods. Cacao traders might have also carried balls of copal tree resin out of the river valleys, as this was the favorite incense of Maya royalty and an important ceremonial offering.

Traders who were particularly ambitious made the journey with live animals originally domesticated far from the Maya area. Archaeological, zooarchaeological, and ancient DNA evidence shows that despite the presence of ocellated turkeys native to the Maya area, many sites have the remains of the Mexican turkey, a species native to the mountains around Mexico City.[12] These birds were transported to the Maya area alive as early as the Preclassic period. Perhaps an older trader, familiar with the long, complicated route through many cultures and regions, and with an extensive

---

[12] Thornton et al. 2012.

network of contacts at each port or large city, had the knowledge needed to make such a long journey as quickly as possible in order to deliver animals in good condition. Even if Ox Ayin, or Three Crocodile, only had to travel to Veracruz, where unusual animals such as hairless dogs and Mexican turkeys were raised, he would still need many days on the water to transport them in his canoe before reaching a southern lowland city on the Usumacinta River or a northern city on the coast. In addition to knowing his route, the safe ports, and the unprotected passes where he might be ambushed, unlike other traders he had to provision his goods along the way, providing them food, water, and shelter. For these reasons Ox Ayin moved as quickly as possible, traveling at night and using the stars to guide his boat. He had as large a crew as possible to keep the boat moving swiftly but he also needed plenty of room for the wicker cages of dogs and turkeys. He had made this journey many times before, and sometimes he carried songbirds from regions outside the Maya area as well. The queen of an isolated and remote riverine city was his best trading patron. She would compensate him well with a delicious feast, a comfortable bed, and plenty of jade for the delivery of these strange creatures. He wasn't sure why she wasn't satisfied with the turkeys from her own forest, but she said they did not have the exquisite flavor of the ones from afar. He was also carrying a special package for a family of traders who lived in this city – the cremated remains of his mentor and friend, an older trader who passed away suddenly far from home. The trader's family would place the remains in an ancestral shrine on the eastern side of the compound and at last he would be at rest.

Unusual marine products made their way to almost all inland centers. In addition to the commodities that every Maya family needed, such as salt, obsidian, and basalt, there were products like jade that were more tightly controlled. Spondylus, found in both the Pacific Ocean and the Caribbean Sea, has a bright orange exterior and a white interior (Figure 6.7). To Maya elite, this shell recalled the primordial sea and its powers of rejuvenation and fertility, as well as the female womb. Large examples were made into royal belts worn by queens to emphasize their powerful role in reproducing the dynasty and all its subjects. Medium-sized examples were often used in ceremonial deposits, with a single jade bead and a small amount of

FIGURE 6.7 Royal earflare carved from spiny bivalve, or spondylus shell, from B23, a royal tomb at Yaxuna. Photo by the author.

powdered red hematite placed inside the two halves of shell. These caches, or small deposits of what we think are precious materials, were placed into royal architecture, and like the queen's belt, they also contained the power of the sea and the earth in talismanic form. Spondylus shell was used for making jewelry for the elite, such as ear spools and ornaments – its bright orange color was a dramatic contrast to jade green. It recalled the sun and its daily rebirth from the sea. Other shells were also traded inland for ornaments, simpler ones of white and gray, when carved into the form of a mask or a skull they enlivened the costumes of dancers or protected small children from harm. Royalty were also in regular need of stingray spines and shark's teeth for ceremonial occasions and to place into royal tombs in order to assure the dead were well equipped for the afterlife and their metaphorical journey back to the sea (which was linked to the underworld). While it is tempting to think that the trade in these obscure ritual tools was more limited than the trade in highland commodities, stingray spines in particular were an essential marker of religious devotion and social status – with thousands of Maya cities in the Classic period, there was a very substantial demand for these marine resources and the traders who provided them were likely kept quite busy. Archaeologists have found artificial sting ray spines carved from deer bone or jade, an indication of both how precious the authentic spines were and the central role of this tool in rituals of self-induced bloodletting.

The enormous coastline of the Maya area was filled with small settlements of fishers, traders, and their families, some of whom were local and some of whom likely traveled from central Mexico, Central America, and perhaps even the Caribbean to benefit from the rich Classic Maya economy and culture. Fishing was a highly productive activity and these populations had surplus food and marine products available to trade with inland centers. They also provided shelter to long-distance traders, some of whom were engaged full-time in the movement of commodities and precious exotic materials from distant inland regions. Circulation of basic necessities such as hard stone for cutting tools and salt was just as essential to Maya society as corn agriculture or ancestor veneration, yet state-sponsored art produced in palace compounds rarely portrays fishers and only occasionally depicts a trader, usually in relation to a king or queen who receives his goods. The ruling ideology of ancient Maya culture was centered on the essential importance of corn agriculture – as a foodstuff, but also as a metaphor for humanity and rulership. While merchants do not often appear in elite art, other lines of evidence suggest coastal and island sites held enormous ritual significance as pilgrimage centers, and the sea was a popular representation of the watery boundary between the living and the dead. It was the balance between inland agriculture and waterborne trade that allowed Maya royalty to live such extravagant lives (Figure 6.8). They were tied to their subjects through a dietary preference for corn but connected to elites elsewhere by the movement of rare materials such as jade and salt that were available only in limited areas. The majority of the population may never have traveled to the coast to see the large trading canoes filled with oarsmen and goods, and coastal people likely did not need to travel inland very often. But their lives were

FIGURE 6.8 Ear ornaments carved in the form of a fish nibbling the roots of waterlilies. University of Miami Special Collections, Jay I. Kislak Collection.

closely linked through the material items they made, harvested, and shared.

Suggested Readings

Andrews, Anthony P. 1983 *Maya Salt Production and Trade.* Tucson: University of Arizona Press.
Cobos, Raphael, ed. 2012 *Arqueologia de la costa de Campeche: La epoca prehispanica.* Merida: Universidad Autonoma de Yucatan.
Hutson, Scott, ed. 2017 *Ancient Maya Commerce: Multidisciplinary Research at Chunchucmil.* Boulder: University Press of Colorado.
McKillop, Heather, and Kazuo Aoyama 2018 Salt and Salted Fish in the Classic Maya Economy from Use-Wear Study of Stone Tools. *Proceedings of the National Academy of Sciences* **115**(43):10948–10952.
Tokovinine, Alexandre, and Dmitri Beliaev 2013 People of the Road: Traders and Travelers in Ancient Maya Words and Images. In *Merchants, Markets, and Exchange in the Pre-Columbian World,* ed. Kenneth Hirth and Joanne Pillsbury, pp. 169–200. Washington, DC: Dumbarton Oaks Research Library and Collection.
Witschey, Walter R. T. 2005 Muyil: An Early Start and a Late Finish in East Coast Settlement. In *Quintana Roo Archaeology,* ed. J. M. Shaw and J. P. Mathews, pp. 127–143. Tucson: University of Arizona Press.

7

Conclusion

Today approximately 6 million people who live in the area explored in this book, but also in a diaspora that includes places like Dallas, Texas, and Vancouver, British Columbia, speak one of the many Mayan languages. Learning Mayan at home is a key component of what it means to be a Maya person in the 21st century, as Maya culture is no longer centered only on the maize agricultural system and dynastic kingship we discovered in earlier chapters. Now Maya people create hip-hop, practice law, win the Nobel prize, and also continue to farm small-scale maize fields where they plant corn, beans, and squash as did their ancestors. They live in the large cities of modern Guatemala and in small villages high in the remote mountain ranges of Belize. They do not agree on what it means to be Maya, a term that originated in the colonial period[1] but was not embraced by people in the area until much later. They do not agree if the name "Maya" is even meaningful to all of them in the same way,[2] other than describing their language family. However, from an outside perspective, Maya culture has both transformed and survived and is an example of one of the most resilient cultures known to scholars of history and culture. But how did we go from royal palaces to hip-hop? What happened between the 9th and 21st centuries? How do Maya people today understand their glorious ancient past – the queens, hieroglyphic

---

[1] Restall 2004.
[2] Castañeda 2004.

panels, and masterpieces of art? What parts of the ancient daily lives we have just discussed are still salient to Maya people today?

***

There are many academic volumes dedicated to the end of the Classic period, the cultural transformation known to the world as the "Maya collapse," the Maya and Mesoamerican cultures of the Postclassic period, the arrival of Spaniards and other European powers, and the subsequent colonial and historic periods. To conclude this volume, we will review these momentous developments briefly, as a coda to the accomplishments of the Classic period and to set the stage for a discussion of how Maya people today interact with their ancient heritage. Anyone interested in ancient Maya culture will benefit from understanding what the Maya endured during the colonial and historic periods, who they are today, and what they find interesting about their past. We do well to remember we are guests in their land, fascinated spectators to a very long and complex historical drama. In this chapter, we briefly review the events following the end of the Classic period and hopefully provide you – the visitor, student, or tourist – with enough context on the present to both deepen your appreciation of the ancient wonders and excite your interest in modern Maya societies.

AFTER THE CLASSIC PERIOD

The Classic period (200–800 CE) is neither the beginning nor the end of Maya civilization. It may not even be the most important or significant era of Maya society, given the tremendous vitality of Maya culture today. However, it is a period of great accomplishments and innovations that has captured the world's attention. Some of the key characteristics of the Classic period were in place hundreds of years earlier, in the Preclassic period, and some aspects that we have discussed in detail in this book persisted through the colonial and historic period to remain important values embraced by many Maya people today. These include rich food traditions, language use, gendered expectations of work, and religious or spiritual practices. And while it is important to remember there is no single Maya culture today, just as there was not a single Maya culture in the past, for many Maya people, the ancient society we read about in earlier chapters continues to inform parts of their lives today. The relationship between past and present is not always an easy one, given the economic pressures of tourism and big agribusiness, to name just two of the arenas where deeply held values clash with modern appetites, yet modern Maya people navigate these intersections in fascinating and successful ways.

You may have heard about a thing called the Maya collapse. Or wondered what happened to the large cities full of merchants, royalty, and farmers. Did they disappear? Did they die from diseases spread by Spanish contact? Did aliens take them to another universe? All of these are reasonable questions (of course that last one isn't, although many have asked!). As stated in Chapter 1 of this book, the chronology of ancient Maya culture is centered on their urban florescence – a word that was used by early Mayanists to describe what they saw as the most interesting period of Maya history. The Classic period is defined by the florescence or apex of cultural accomplishments as noted by archaeologists, historians, and other scholars of ancient societies. These include impressive architectural accomplishments, a rich literate tradition, artistic masterpieces, and a large number of urban centers where this cultural production occurred and was consumed. Consequently, when early scholars saw archaeological sites that had smaller and less well-constructed architecture, they immediately compared those sites with the apex sites and judged them "decadent" (the actual word they used for what we now label as the Postclassic period). The study of cultures has progressed significantly since that time, and we now understand that cultures are neither more nor less complex than each other; the complexity is just expressed in more or less visible (to late modern Western eyes) ways. The smaller and more sparse cities of the Postclassic Maya world are the result of the evolution of Maya culture to adapt to a new set of challenges and the unique opportunities of the Postclassic world. Their complexity was expressed in less visible means, perhaps in cultural forms that did not preserve as well as earlier architecture or art, or perhaps in social relationships that did not require materialization.

Now that we have established that complexity cannot be subtracted or evaporate from a cultural tradition, we can explore what happened in the Maya world after the Classic kingdoms and prior to the arrival of the Spanish, a period of nearly 600 years. Scholars use the phrase "Terminal Classic" for the time period of 800–1100 CE – and it is just what it sounds like – a 300 year period in which many of the dramatic aspects of Classic society came to an end. Again, this was not a conclusion in the sense we describe a terminal illness as the end of life; it was not a final chapter but rather an internal response to an array of very significant forces.[3] Perhaps most significant was Maya history itself. By 800 CE, Maya settlements had grown in number and density for nearly a thousand years. That's 1,000 years of planting corn, beans, and squash in the same soils, using the same wells for drinking, and disposing of waste in the same areas. Few civilizations last more than a thousand years without major transformations. Another force that has received a lot of attention in the media is the evidence for widespread droughts in the 9th century, especially in the southern Maya area. These droughts must have exacerbated all other existing tensions over land, agricultural productivity, and the excesses of the elite. The majority of southern Maya urban centers were abandoned in the 9th century, some with dramatic evidence for conflict and siege warfare, others with no indication of why, other than poorly maintained, crumbling buildings and an absence of new stelae or inscriptions. Simultaneously, many Maya cities in the northern lowlands were growing, and struggling to provide new houses, palaces, and goods with the resources available. In the midst of this chaos and change, the huge Maya city of Chichen Itza arises on the northern plains of Yucatan, an attempt to reinvent urban life around a new model of pan-Mesoamerican economic and ritual connections. The Maya rulers of Chichen Itza were well connected to important cities outside the Maya area and proclaimed their political power based on participation in a network that shared goods and ideas from as far away as the American Southwest and Lower Central America. Never had Maya rulers had access to goods from such distances, and these connections fueled a population boom at Chichen Itza that was dramatic, but short-lived – by 1200 CE this city was largely abandoned. The Terminal Classic period is a time of paradox – decline and growth, silence and activity. And this period is the beginning of a great transformation away from dynastic kingship and its land claims.

We use the term "Postclassic" to describe the subsequent 400 years because the Maya world was an entirely different place at this time.

---

[3] Demarest et al. 2023.

Aspects of Classic Maya culture can be discerned in the Postclassic period, but social and political life were so thoroughly reinvented that it is better described as something altogether new. This reinvention was caused by a dramatic geopolitical shift, with the rise of the Aztec Empire in central Mexico around 1250 CE. The weight of Mesoamerican power was now firmly centered in the Basin of Mexico, where modern Mexico City is located. Many cities across Mesoamerica that were networked through trade and religious activity during the Terminal Classic period shifted their focus to relations with the Aztecs and their allies. This left the Maya area on the edge of the major political and economic forces at work in the region. The ideas and goods that had propped up the leaders and citizens of Chichen Itza in earlier centuries did not flow as freely in the Maya world now, and only those few settlements that interacted as trading nodes shared ideas and iconography with central Mexico. Maya people reoccupied small settlements on the east coast of the Yucatan peninsula as trading outposts, and refurbished the buildings with new murals, sculpture, and artifacts that proclaimed their connections to the great merchants of central Mexico. Those Maya people who still believed in the idea of urbanism fled to another reinvented city, this time at the Maya settlement of Mayapan. Many aspects of the Maya urban tradition continued at Mayapan with palaces, temples, and pyramids supported by a large semi-urban and rural population of farmers.[4] And as in earlier times, the leaders of Mayapan were constantly in conflict with neighboring polities. Those Maya people who did not want to participate in maritime trade or urban life within a walled compound joined their families who had earlier fled for the forest. In these abandoned lands people could farm and hunt on a small scale, and while there was conflict over access to the best lands, most rural Maya people were free of the taxes and tribute Postclassic lords demanded. Some made journeys to abandoned cities during the Postclassic period and built small shrines from the stones of Classic period buildings. No one wanted to live in the crumbling cities any longer, but these shrines kept people connected to their distant ancestors and to the memories of the Classic period. By the end of

[4] Masson and Peraza Lope 2014.

the Postclassic period the Maya world fragmented into a landscape of small polities, with the majority of the population living in small independent hamlets.

Fragmentation was an astute survival technique that allowed Maya people to endure the failure of state-level political leadership and the harsh price it exacted on the environment. By returning to small-scale farming, Maya people relied on a deep Indigenous knowledge of their tropical world and, in effect, traded the exotic goods and splendor of urban life for a sustainable, if more simple, rural existence. The lack of centralized Maya political power was of tremendous benefit to the Maya when Spaniards arrived in the Yucatan peninsula and found no emperor or single authority to subdue. The first documented contact between Maya people and Europeans occurred in 1502, during the fourth voyage of Christopher Columbus, when his brother sighted a huge wooden dugout canoe filled with traders, cotton cloth, ceramic vessels, and cacao off the coast of Honduras. The colonial period began with Bartholomew Columbus' next act – he seized the goods he wanted as well as the captain of the trading canoe. There was no attempt at the mediation or negotiation that Indigenous traders, many of whom traveled with the protection of state-level diplomatic sanction, might have expected.

Nine years later, at the next encounter with Europeans, Maya expectations had adjusted to the new realities of the time, and when ten Spanish shipwreck victims washed ashore on the island of Cozumel, the Spanish captain and four of his men were immediately killed. A local Maya lord took two others, Geronimo de Aguilar and Gonzalo Guerrero, as prisoners and enslaved them. Aguilar was a Franciscan friar and the Maya lord took pleasure in tempting him with Maya wives. Aguilar had a skill for languages and eventually was rescued by Hernando Cortes in order to accompany Cortes' expedition as a translator in service to the conquest of the Aztec capital. Guerrero, a sailor, embraced Maya culture, earned his release from slavery, and lived the rest of his life in Yucatan, fathering three children with his Maya wife.

Following these isolated incidents, and as Spanish exploration of the New World gained momentum, Maya people increasingly lived under siege. Only those in the deepest parts of the rainforest were free from contact with Spanish conquistadors hungry for treasure, of which there was virtually none, given the Maya preference for jade over gold or silver and the subsequent arrival of Spanish ecclesiasticals looking to save native souls. Spanish ships soon arrived on both the west and east coasts of the Yucatan peninsula, where they were met by Maya war canoes and armed warriors. The Maya inhabitants of Cozumel, living under the protection of a local lord who was engaged in trade with the Aztec, fled from Spanish explorers. This allowed the first Christian cross to be erected in the Maya world on Cozumel, in 1519. After a defeat in the waters of the Gulf of Mexico, a Maya lord offered the Spanish captain the small amount of gold he had, food, clothing, and a group of Maya women to help cook and care for the Spanish men. Among those women was a noblewoman captured from her home in central Mexico and enslaved in the Maya lowlands where she learned to speak multiple Mayan languages. She too had linguistic talent and would become the most famous translator in the history of the New World. Known today as La Malinche, she was originally named Malintzin, and later took the Spanish name Marina.[5]

Although native documents make clear that Maya people framed the arrival of Spaniards as yet one more incursion from the west, familiar as they were with outsiders who spoke different languages from other parts of Mesoamerica, Spanish technology – canons, guns, soldiers on horseback – was substantially more threating for the Maya than weapons brought by previous invaders. When Maya people engaged with the Spanish armed forces they often did not emerge victorious. When they fled into the interior of their territory and forced their enemies to engage them there, they had a substantial tactical advantage. The absence of a single Maya king or emperor was also a strategic advantage and allowed Maya people living in different areas to resist the single political conquest suffered by the Aztecs in central Mexico or the Inca in Peru. Over the 16th century there were hundreds of revolts and ambushes within the Maya area, as Spaniards attempted to control the land they believed would ultimately yield the wealth of the Aztec or Inca empires. But in less than 100 years, the covetous conquistadors learned there were no substantial mines or warehouses full of gold and silver in these lands. Other than slaves,

[5] Jager 2015.

cotton, and beeswax, the Maya area held little of value to the Spanish enterprise. Thus unlike central Mexico or Peru for the next few hundred years, the Maya area was largely left in the hands of the church and a few powerful landholders until the 19th century.

Franciscan fervor to convert the Maya was unrelenting, and sometimes brutal. A few friars pleaded to Spain to protect Maya people from other Spaniards. More typical of the period were great displays of colonial power and dominance, and ruthless clerics like Bishop Landa burned hundreds of native books filled with hieroglyphic texts. Writing in the Maya script, worship of Maya gods, and performance of the rituals long practiced to ensure a sufficient harvest and protection from destructive natural forces such as earthquakes or hurricanes were all declared heretical. Yet conversion to Christianity was slow, as many Maya people remained far from the Spanish cities built atop Classic period platforms with ancient carved stone. For many Maya people living in the interior of the southern lowlands, or deep in the remote mountains of the Maya highlands, Spanish contact was avoided whenever possible and life persisted according to the rhythms of agricultural cycles and family. In areas frequented by Europeans, Maya people were rounded up and forced to live under supervision, with dramatically less freedom of movement, belief, or daily activity. Tightly controlled, Maya people living in these nucleated settlements were forced to provide extremely large quantities of goods and services to support the Spanish way of life. Again, the only viable means of resistance was to flee these settlements and move deeper into the interior. Some noble Maya families allied themselves with the new invaders, and remained politically influential well into the colonial period. Members of these families learned to read and write Spanish and Latin from church leaders, and assisted friars with conversion of Maya people. A famous member of this class is Gaspar Antonio Chi, a Yucatec Maya man who became the assistant to Bishop Landa, a Franciscan who, in his later life, compiled one of the few Spanish accounts of 16th-century Maya life. Chi likely wrote many of the passages describing Maya culture that Landa claimed as his own.[6]

---

[6] Restall et al. 2023.

The subsequent centuries of the historical period saw the introduction of European plants and livestock in the Maya area, which permanently changed Maya economic practices and foodways. Maya people adopted horses, cattle, and swine enthusiastically, as well as plant foods such as sugarcane, citrus, and coffee. Unfortunately, many of these crops were grown on plantations where conditions were just as brutal and dangerous as the better-known plantations of the Caribbean. Living under the control of wealthy Spaniards, Maya people became debt peons, enslaved on large-scale haciendas that grew sugarcane, henequen (a rope fiber that dominated the world market prior to plastics), and coffee. The 18th and 19th centuries saw the worst health disparities known in Maya civilization, due to the combination of European diseases, severe workloads, extreme poverty, and crowded living conditions.[7]

The independence movements of young nation-states within the Maya world brought a patchwork of improvements, as Indigenous cultures were no longer enslaved but merely subject to the control of powerful criollos, those born in the Americas of Spanish descent. The Mexican War of Independence began in 1808, with Spain eventually surrendering political control of Mexico in 1821. That same year Honduras became independent, and Guatemala began its own independence movement, with freedom from Spain effectively achieved in 1840. Belize remained a colony of Great Britain until – remarkably – 1981. Scholars often consider the Spanish American wars of independence to be "civil wars" between different factions of native elites, many of whom had learned to reject Indigenous culture, even if they shared Indigenous heritage. Maya people benefited from independence from Spain in minor ways: with independence, technically they enjoyed freedom of religion and freedom from enforced labor; however, with the seizure of church lands, wealthy criollos grew even wealthier and their need for manual laborers only increased. Throughout the Maya area, in the 19th and 20th centuries, Maya people spent their daily lives living in impoverished conditions resulting from the extreme economic and political inequalities that characterized most of Latin America. While wealthy Latinos were

[7] Meyers 2005.

often of Indigenous ancestry, their ascent within Latino society required a rejection of Indigenous lifeways and a full embrace of European cultural practices. These cultural expectations rested in the cruel bedrock of widespread racism, and Maya people spent much of the late 19th and early 20th centuries repressed and silenced by the nation-states they were forced to live under.

At the turn of the 20th century, business owners from the United States joined their European kin and began investing heavily in the Maya area, growing fruit and coffee on large plantations. The most well-known of these was the United Fruit Company, which by 1930 had become the largest employer in Central America. Early multinational corporations like the United Fruit Company exerted tremendous influence over the national politics of young Central American nations, and the United States government, particularly the CIA, used such businesses as a means to control these governments. In 1954, through its international business and political connections, the CIA deposed a democratically elected president of Guatemala and installed a pro-business military dictatorship.[8] The neocolonial actions of the United States at this time set the stage for one of the darkest periods in Maya history, the long and painful civil war of Guatemala, which lasted from 1960 to 1996. US-backed Guatemalan military action against the mostly Maya population of Guatemala cost the lives of approximately 200,000 people. The memoir of a Maya woman from the highlands of Guatemala who grew up during the civil war, *I, Rigoberto Menchu*, drew international attention to the plight of Maya people and Menchu was awarded the Nobel Peace Prize in 1992.[9] Maya people played key roles in the peace process, which eventually resulted in a final agreement in 1996.

Today over 6 million people living in the Maya area or within the diaspora speak a Maya language. The close of the 20th century brought a gradual improvement in civil rights for Maya people throughout the region as a result of their demand for better treatment, and an increasing representation of Maya people in the local and national governments of Mexico, Guatemala, Belize, and Honduras. More Maya speakers hold positions of influence in their

---

[8] Talbot 2015.
[9] Menchu 1984.

countries as doctors, professors, lawyers, and artists than at any time in the last 500 years. Yet many Maya people still live in disadvantaged conditions that are largely the result of attitudes, prejudices, and inequalities that originate in the colonial and historic periods. So while the Maya did not disappear in the way many documentaries might imply, they left their cities, endured a violent invasion, had their beliefs and lifeways criminalized, and saw many of their kin enslaved on plantations or slaughtered during war. Their story is much more complicated than a disappearance, much less mysterious, and much more gruesome. It is a testament to how, even when treated as inhuman, people can survive and resist the domination of those who abuse positions of authority. Maya civilization is alive and flourishing despite the extreme measures taken to ensure that would never happen – the forced conversions, the physical abuse, the deprivation. And yet today, Maya people speak their original language with some Spanish loan words; they create literature in that language and art in keeping with their own aesthetics; and they raise families where they perpetuate the calendar system, agricultural practices, recipes, and prayers that originated over 2,000 years ago.

MODERN MAYA PERSPECTIVES ON THEIR CLASSIC HERITAGE

The primary place I do field research is in Yaxunah, a small village of Yucatec Maya–speaking people in the middle of the Yucatan peninsula of Mexico. I was fortunate enough to be invited to join an archaeological project there in 1989, and while I directed projects in other parts of the Maya area for many years, I returned to Yaxunah in the 2010s to continue collaborating with the Maya people who live there to recover aspects of their ancient heritage. Along the way I learned, as many other scholars in the field of archaeology have realized, that just because an aspect of ancient Maya culture is interesting to late modern Westerners, does not mean it is also interesting to Maya people. More broadly speaking, over the past twenty years the field of archaeology has become much more sensitive to the interests of descendant communities, those people who are invested culturally, geographically, or historically in the archaeological materials academic archaeologists study. It is fascinating to scholars of my generation that our research now shows archaeology was built on the assumption that there are artifacts or objects of universal appeal, but we now acknowledge that such an abstract concept as "universal appeal" does not exist. Not every site should be explored, not every beautiful object should be studied, and in fact not everyone agrees on what is beautiful, important, or available to study. My academic predecessors perceived no limits on the questions they could ask, and the price they paid for that was a disengagement with the descendant communities where they conducted research. Today's scholars seek to collaborate on questions of interest and significance to Maya people, knowing not all Maya people agree on what is interesting and significant. Our scientific investigations are vastly improved by asking questions about what is of interest to the communities where we work, rather than acting in isolation from their interests.

Maya people today are interested in Classic period foodways and use their culinary heritage to generate tourism. In Yaxunah, people are very interested in Maya foodways, and one of my main lines of research is recovering information about local food heritage, sharing it with the community members who are interested, and helping them advocate for the role that they wish to have in local culinary tourism. Over the many years that the archaeological projects in Yaxunah excavated commoner houses, elite tombs, burials of all kinds, and other strange and wonderful materials, I noticed a persistent interest in the tools and areas ancient people used to prepare food. When I discussed the stone metate we excavated with one of the field crew from the village, he mentioned a similar tool used by his grandmother. When we visited the village for special occasions and ate piles of handmade tortillas, I recalled all the isotopic evidence that Classic Maya people also survived on corn. When a local group of women formed a food tourism cooperative, they asked for information about what ancient Maya people ate, and now they factor that data into the stories they tell the foodies and tourists who travel to the village in search of an authentic Maya taco.[10]

Modern Maya people are interested in the history of their language and its evolution, and they use hieroglyphics to strengthen their identity as Maya speakers. For twenty-five years, workshops have been

---

[10] Ardren 2018.

held in Guatemala City; Valladolid, Mexico; Belmopan, Belize; and other cities with sizable Maya populations, where Maya-speaking people study how to read and write Maya hieroglyphics. Originally started by Western academic epigraphers and linguists who worked with Maya communities and at the invitation of those communities, these workshops have trained hundreds of Maya epigraphers in the written language of their ancestors.[11] Many of these Maya students have become instructors and professional scholars of the inscriptions. Due to the structural inequalities that linger in Latin America long after the colonial and historic periods, the vast majority of Maya-speaking people have had little access to the information generated by the scholarly study of their ancient language and culture. High school and university-level education are not accessible to many Maya people who live in the more rural, remote, or poor areas of Mexico, Guatemala, Belize, or Honduras. Given the rapid pace of hieroglyphic decipherment, and the small number of scholars initially involved, even Maya people who entered university did not have ready access to the texts written in the Classic period. This changed in the mid-1990s when a group of professors from the United States, Mexico, Guatemala, and Europe asked Maya speakers to help them understand the texts. In turn these scholars were invited by Maya speakers to expand the conversation about ancient Maya writing with a series of workshops that have continued ever since. Native Maya speakers have an intuitive grasp on the grammar of the inscriptions, and easily identify the plants and animals mentioned in the inscriptions and related art as elements of their natural world, something urban Western scholars might struggle to do. The revitalization of hieroglyphic literacy has played an important role in civil rights movements such as the pan-Maya movement, which fights the political marginalization of Maya people across the Guatemala-Mexico border. Maya speakers seeking to protect and restore the Maya language have found inspiration and ammunition for their cause in the greater access to 2,000 years of Maya literature that hieroglyphic literacy enables.

Modern Maya people are passionate about their deep agricultural legacy and the way ancient crops remain a potent element of their

---

[11] Mooney 1996.

lives today.[12] Maya people living in the Yucatan peninsula have a long and rich history of organic farming and beekeeping that dates directly to the Classic period when apiculture was an essential component of the complex agricultural system needed to support hundreds of thousands of people. Maya beekeepers have preserved their knowledge of native bees, such as the stingless xunan kab (*Melipona beecheii*) while also mastering the skills needed to tend European honeybees (*Apis mellifera*). Today, Mexico is the third largest producer of organic honey in the world.[13] The vast majority of that organic honey is produced by small-scale Indigenous farmers who sell to wholesalers as part of their mixed subsistence strategy that combines apiculture with milpa farming and other Indigenous traditions. In the last decade, Monsanto and other multinational corporations have sought to enter the Mexican agricultural system, which in some parts of the country is as mechanized and massive in scale as agriculture has become in the United States. When the Mexican government granted Monsanto hundreds of thousands of hectares of land to test a genetically modified strain of soybean, Maya farmers in Yucatan and Campeche noticed an impact on their honey production.

Bees that forage on genetically modified crops are no longer considered organic by Mexican standards, and pollen from genetically modified plants can travel for miles. Modern Maya farmers objected to the introduction of genetically modified seeds, and joined forces with scientists and activists to argue against GMO agriculture. Objection to the introduction of GMO corn was a major issue around which Maya people of Chiapas, Mexico, organized during the Zapatista uprising of the 1990s.[14] In 2015, the Mexican Supreme Court recognized the inherent rights of Maya people to a traditional way of life and banned Monsanto and other similar companies from cultivating GMO soybeans in the states of Yucatan and Campeche. At the same time a Mexican appeals court upheld a 2013 decision to ban the sale of GMO corn within Mexican borders. Although these

---

[12] Ernesto Hernández-López, "Fighting GMO Corn, for Mexico's Soul," Latino Rebels, September 16, 2020, www.latinorebels.com/2020/09/16/fightinggmocorn.

[13] "Rising Demand for Organic Foods in Mexico," Wisconsin Economic Development, January 1, 2018, https://wedc.org/export/market-intelligence/posts/rising-demand-organic-foods-mexico.

[14] Brown 2013.

Conclusion

agreements are regularly violated, a movement of Maya and other Indigenous people has arisen around the chant, "Sin maíz, no hay país" (Without corn, there is no nation), which invokes the deep spiritual connection Maya people have with corn as a foodstuff, ritual substance, and way of life. Maya activists deploy scientific information that archaeologists generate that Mexico is the site where corn was originally domesticated. These activists warn that once GMO corn is introduced, its pollen will spread throughout the country, endangering the many native and heritage varieties still grown. The current President of Mexico has promised to make GMO corn illegal but has yet to take action on this promise.

Modern Maya people are interested in the spiritual legacy of the Classic past, and how it can inspire new art, advance their civil rights, and support the reclamation of their identities. Tzutun Kan is a hip hop artist from the Maya highlands of Guatemala, and he performs in the Mayan languages of Tz'utujil, Kakchiquel, and K'iche', the language used to record the adventures of the Maya Hero Twins in the Popul Vuh. He is part of a group of rapper artists known as Balam Ajpu, Maya for Jaguar Warriors, who teach hip-hop as a way to encourage young people to retain Mayan languages. His first album, which came out in 2016, has twenty songs, one for each day in the Mayan calendar.[15] Tzutun and his collaborators acknowledge that hip-hop came to Guatemala originally in a form very similar to what is performed in the United States, but around 2010, it started to evolve under the influence of what they call GuateMaya. Their style has eclectic sampling from other music genres like cumbia and merengue or any music played well that has a social conscience. Tzutun and the other members of Balam Ajpu use hip-hop as a powerful tool for political and cultural resistance, and openly state that their culture has always been oppressed, so to do anything that reaches a wider audience is, by definition, a political act of resistance. Their songs are titled after materials and animals from their homeland that have a deep resonance with Maya people, such as obsidian and kan, the Maya word for snake. Videos on Soundcloud are illustrated with artifacts

---

[15] Martha Pskowski, "Meet Balam Ajpu, a Mayan Hip-Hop Trio That Proves Indigenous Art Transcends Folklore," Remezcla.com, https://remezcla.com/features/music/balam-ajpu-profile.

from Classic period Maya sites, animals that appear in Classic and modern Maya art, and performers dressed in the feathers and costumes of Classic period Maya kings. Their lyrics draw on Indigenous Maya spirituality as a form of resistance to Western culture, and the group has incorporated aspects of Maya ceremonies in their live performances. Tzutun is just one of a growing number of Maya hip-hop artists, with others in Guatemala and various parts of Mexico, rapping in Mayan languages. They feel hip-hop has always given a voice to the most oppressed people, and that's why it's the right medium for them now.

The journey from royal palaces to hip-hop has been treacherous, but modern Maya people draw from the past in ways that late modern Westerners might find hard to understand. Elements of Classic culture that we discussed in detail in this volume, such as the importance of corn agriculture and the animated spirit of natural places, remain vital elements of modern Maya life. The archaeological sites where scholars perform research are sources of inspiration to some modern Maya people, who draw on the data and imagery generated. The Classic culture does not speak to all modern Maya people, just as it does not speak to all students of ancient cultures. But the remains of the Classic period are a vital part of modern Maya cultural production, as well as the cultural tourism industry, the advertising industry, and educational institutions such as museums, university curricula, and cultural centers. The accomplishments of the ancient Maya are not locked in the past, 1,000 years ago; they are present in modern Maya and non-Maya lives today whether we learned Maya at home or are reading about this important civilization for the first time. Images from the Classic period appear in travel brochures, on ice cream containers, in the news, and in the art or music we consume. The daily lives of ancient Maya people left a tremendous record for us to explore, and we are fortunate to have access to their lessons, accomplishments, and misadventures. Let us be careful and thoughtful stewards, mindful of our place as guests in another country, in another culture. And as we carry on with our daily lives, perhaps the distance between what we do and the lives of someone in the ancient city of Coba, will be reduced.

Bibliography

Ak'abal, Humberto 1999 *Poems I Brought Down from the Mountain*. St. Paul, MN: Nineties Press.

Anderson, E. N., and Felix Medina Tzuc 2005 *Animals and the Maya in Southeast Mexico*. Tucson: University of Arizona Press.

Andrews, Anthony P. 1983 *Maya Salt Production and Trade*. Tucson: University of Arizona Press.

— 2008 Facilidades portuarias mayas. In *El territorio maya: Memoria de la quinta mesa redonda de Palenque*, ed. Rodrido Liendo Stuardo, pp. 15–40. Mexico City: Instituto Nacional de Antropologia e Historia.

Andrews, Anthony P., Tomas Gallareta Negron, Fernando Robles Castellano, Rafael Cobos Palma, and Pura Cervera Rivero 1988 Isla Cerritos: An Itza Trading Port on the North Coast of Yucatan, Mexico. *National Geographic Research* 4(2):196–207.

Ardren, Traci 2018 Now Serving Maya Heritage: Culinary Tourism in Yaxunah, Yucatan, Mexico. *Food and Foodways* 26(4):290–312.

Astor-Aguilera, Miguel 2020 Maya Rites, Rituals, and Ceremonies. In *The Maya World*, eds. Scott Hutson and Traci Ardren, pp. 648–668. London: Routledge.

Aveni, Anthony 2001 *Skywatchers of Ancient Mexico*. Austin: University of Texas Press.

Aveni, Anthony E., and Anne S. Dowd 2017 E Groups: Astronomy, Alignments, and Maya Cosmology. In *Maya E Groups: Calendars, Astronomy, and Urbanism in the Early Lowlands*, ed. David Freidel et al., pp. 75–94. Gainesville: University of Florida Press.

Barrett, Rusty 2015 Mayan Language Revitalization, Hip Hop, and Ethnic Identity in Guatemala. *Language and Communication* 47(2016):144–153.

Beach, Tim, Sheryl Luzzadder-Beach, Nicholas Dunning, and Samantha Krause 2020 Paleoecology, Soil, and Water in Maya History. In *The Maya World*, eds. Scott Hutson and Traci Ardren, pp. 229–249. London: Routledge.

Bricker, Harvey M., and Victoria R. Bricker 2011 *Astronomy in the Maya Codices*. Philadelphia: American Philosophical Society.

Bricker, Victoria R., Anthony F. Aveni, and Harvey M. Bricker 2014 Deciphering the Handwriting on the Wall: Some Astronomical

Interpretations of the Recent Discoveries at Xultun, Guatemala. *Latin American Antiquity* 25(2):152–169.

Brown, Peter 2013 Maya Mother Seeds in Resistance of Highland Chiapas in Defense of Native Corn. In *Seeds of Resistance, Seeds of Hope: Place and Agency in the Conservation of Biodiversity*, ed. Virginia D. Nazarea, pp. 151–176. Tucson: University of Arizona Press.

Callaghan, Michael 2016 Observations on Invisible Producers: Engendering Pre-Columbian Maya Ceramic Production. In *Gendered Labor in Specialized Economies*, eds. S. Kelly and T. Ardren, pp. 267–300. Boulder: University Press of Colorado.

Carter, Nicolas, and Mallory E. Matsumoto 2020 The Epigraphy of Ancient Maya Food and Drink. In *Her Cup for Sweet Cacao: Food in Ancient Maya Society*, ed. T. Ardren, pp. 87–123. Austin: University of Texas Press.

Castañeda, Quetzil 2004 "We Are Not Indigenous!": An Introduction to the Maya Identity of Yucatan. *Journal of Latin American Anthropology* 9(1):36–63.

Chase, Diane, Patricia McAnany, and Jeremy Sabloff 2017 Epilogue: E Groups and Their Significance to the Ancient Maya. In *Maya E Groups: Calendars, Astronomy, and Urbanism in the Early Lowlands*, ed. David Freidel et al., pp. 578–582. Gainesville: University Press of Florida.

Chinchilla Mazariegos, Oswaldo 2017 *Art and Myth of the Ancient Maya*. New Haven, CT: Yale University Press.

Cobos, Raphael, ed. 2012 *Arqueologia de la costa de Campeche: La epoca prehispanica*. Merida: Universidad Autonoma de Yucatan.

Coe, Michael D., and Stephen D. Houston 2015 *The Maya*. New York: Thames and Hudson.

Coe, Michael D., and Justin Kerr 1998 *The Art of the Maya Scribe*. New York: Harry N. Abrams.

Coe, Michael D., Mary Miller, Stephen Houston, and Karl Taube 2015 *The Fourth Maya Codex*. Maya Archaeology 3. San Francisco, CA: Precolumbia Mesoweb Press.

Coe, Michael D., and Mark Van Stone 2001 *Reading the Maya Glyphs*. New York: Thames and Hudson.

Cuevas Cob, Briceida 1998 *Je' bix k'in/Como el sol*. Mexico City: Instituto Nacional Indigenista.

Cunningham-Smith, Petra, Ashley E. Sharpe, Arianne Boileau, Erin Kennedy Thornton, and Kitty F. Emery 2020 Food, Friend, or Offering: Exploring the Role of Maya Dogs in the Zooarchaeological Record. In *Her Cup for Cacao: Food in Ancient Maya Society*, ed. T. Ardren, pp. 161–187. Austin: University of Texas Press.

Demarest, Arthur A., Prudence M. Rice, and Don S. Rice, eds. 2004 *The Terminal Classic in the Maya Lowlands: Collapse, Transition, and Transformation*. Boulder: University Press of Colorado.

Dunning, Nicolas, Timothy Beach, Elizabeth Graham, David Lentz, and Sheryl Luzzadder-Beach 2018 Getting to the Grain: The Domestication of *Zea mays* in Mesoamerica and Beyond. In *The Archaeology of Caribbean*

and *Circum-Caribbean Farmers (5000 BC–AD 1500)*, ed. Basil A. Reid, pp. 329–352. New York: Routledge.
Folan, William 1992 Calakmul, Campeche: A Centralized Urban Administrative Center in the Northern Peten. *World Archaeology* 24:58–168.
Ford, Anabel, and Ronald Nigh 2015 *The Maya Forest Garden: Eight Millennia of Sustainable Cultivation of the Tropical Woodlands*. New York: Routledge.
Freidel, David A., Arlen F. Chase, Anne S. Dowd, and Jerry Murdock, eds. 2017 *Maya E Groups: Calendars, Astronomy, and Urbanism in the Early Lowlands*. Gainesville: University Press of Florida.
Frischmann, Donald H., and Wildernain Villegas, eds. 2016 *U suut t'aan: U t'aan maaya ajts'übo'ob tu lu'umil Quintana Roo/El retorno de la palabra: Voces de escritores mayas en Quintana Roo/The Return of Our Word: Voices of Mayan Writers from Quintana Roo*. Mexico City: Plumas Negras Editorial.
Gillespie, Susan D. 1991 Ballgames and Boundaries. In *The Mesoamerican Ballgame*, eds. Vernon Scarborough and David Wilcox, pp. 317–345. Tucson: University of Arizona Press.
Glover, Jeffrey 2012 The Yalahau Region: A Study of Ancient Maya Sociopolitical Organization. *Ancient Mesoamerica* 23(2012):271–295.
Götz, Christopher M. 2012 La fauna vertebrada arqueologica de la costa campechana: El caso de Champoton. In *Arqueologia de la costa de Campeche: La época prehispánica*, ed. Rafael Cobos, pp. 97–126. Merida: Ediciones de la Universidad Autonoma de Yucatan.
Guenter, Stanley 2014 The Queen of Coba: A Reanalysis of the Macanxoc Stelae. In *The Archaeology of Yucatan*, ed. T. Stanton, pp. 395–421. Oxford: Archaeopress.
Guenter, Stanley P., and David A. Freidel 2005 Warriors and Rulers: Royal Women of the Classic Maya. In *Gender in Cross Cultural Perspective*, 4th ed., eds. C. Brettell and C. Sargent, pp. 74–80. Upper Saddle River, NJ: Prentice Hall.
Gutierrez, Eugenia 2016 Reinas y guerreras mayas en inscripciones del periodo Clásico. Paper presented at the X Congreso Internacioal de Mayistas, Izamal, Mexico. June 2016.
Guzman, Gaston 2008 Hallucinogenic Mushrooms in Mexico: An Overview. *Economic Botany* 62(3):404–412.
Halperin, Christina 2014 *Maya Figurines: Intersections between State and Household*. Austin: University of Texas Press.
Hammond, Norman, and Jeremy Bauer 2001 A Preclassic Maya Sweatbath at Cuello, Belize. *Antiquity* 75(290):683–684.
Hendon, Julia A. 1997 Women's Work, Women's Space and Women's Status among the Classic Period Maya Elite of the Copan Valley, Honduras. In *Women in Prehistory*, eds. C. Claassen and R. A. Joyce, pp. 33–46. Philadelphia: University of Pennsylvania Press.
Houston, Stephen D. 1996 Symbolic Sweatbaths of the Maya: Architectural Meaning in the Cross Group at Palenque, Mexico. *Latin American Antiquity* 7(2):132–151.

Houston, Stephen D., John Robertson, and David Stuart 2000 The Language of Classic Maya Inscriptions. *Current Anthropology* 41:321–356.

Houston, Stephen D., and David Stuart 1989 *The Way Glyph: Evidence for "Co-essences" among the Classic Maya*. Vol. 30. Barnardsville, NC: Center for Maya Research.

  1992 On Maya Hieroglyphic Literacy. *Current Anthropology* 33(5):589–593.

Hurst, Heather 2020 Maya Mural Painting. In *The Maya World*, ed. Scott Hutson and T. Ardren, pp. 578–598. London: Routledge.

Hutson, Scott R. 2010 *Dwelling, Identity, and the Maya: Relational Archaeology at Chunchucmil*. Walnut Creek, CA: AltaMira Press.

  2016 *The Ancient Urban Maya: Neighborhoods, Inequality, and Built Form*. Gainesville: University Press of Florida.

  2017 ed. *Ancient Maya Commerce: Multidisciplinary Research at Chunchucmil*. Boulder: University Press of Colorado.

  2020 Inequality and Social Groups. In *The Maya World*, ed. Scott Hutson and T. Ardren, pp. 407–423. London: Routledge.

Isendahl, Christian 2012 Agro-Urban Landscapes: The Example of Maya Lowland Cities. *Antiquity* 86:1112–1125.

Jager, Rebecca K. 2015 *Malinche, Pocahontas, and Sacagawea: Indian Women as Cultural Intermediaries and National Symbols*. Norman: University of Oklahoma Press.

Johnston, Kevin J. 2001 Broken Fingers: Classic Maya Scribe Capture and Polity Consolidation. *Antiquity* 75:373–381.

King, Eleanor M., ed. 2015 *The Ancient Maya Marketplace: The Archaeology of Transient Space*. Tucson: University of Arizona Press.

Kovacevich, Brigitte 2014 The Inalienability of Jades in Mesoamerica. *Archaeological Papers of the American Anthropological Association* 23(1):95–111.

Looper, Matthew G. 2009 *To Be Like Gods: Dance in Ancient Maya Civilization*. Austin: University of Texas Press.

Lucero, Lisa 2006 *Water and Ritual: The Rise and Fall of Classic Maya Rulers*. Austin: University Press of Texas.

Martin, Simon 2020 *Ancient Maya Politics: A Political Anthropology of the Classic Period 150–900 CE*. Cambridge: Cambridge University Press.

McAnany, Patricia A 2013 *Living with the Ancestors: Kinship and Kingship in Ancient Maya Society*. Cambridge: Cambridge University Press.

McAnany, Patricia A., and Satoru Murata 2006 From Chocolate Pots to Maya Gold: Belizean Cacao Farmers through the Ages. In *Chocolate in Mesoamerica: A Cultural History of Cacao*, ed. Cameron McNeil, pp. 429–450. Gainesville: University Press of Florida.

McKillop, Heather, and Kazuo Aoyama 2018 Salt and Salted Fish in the Classic Maya Economy from Use-Wear Study of Stone Tools. *Proceedings of the National Academy of Sciences* 115(43):10948–10952.

McKillop, Heather, Elizabeth Sills, and Vincent Cellucci 2014 The Ancient Maya Canoe Paddle and the Canoe from Paynes Creek National Park, Belize. *Research Reports in Belizean Archaeology* 11:297–306.

Mansell, Eugenia, Robert Tykot, David Freidel, Bruce Dahlin, and Traci Ardren 2006 Early to Terminal Classic Maya Diet in the Northern Lowlands of the Yucatán (Mexico). In *Histories of Maize: Multidisciplinary Approaches to the Prehistory, Biogeography, Domestication, and Evolution of Maize*, eds. J. E. Staller, R. H. Tykot, and B. F. Benz, pp. 173–185. New York: Academic Press.

Masson, Marilyn A., David A. Freidel, and Arthur Demarest, eds. 2020 *The Real Business of Ancient Maya Economies: From Farmers' Fields to Rulers' Realms*. Gainesville: University Press of Florida.

Masson, Marilyn, and Carlos Peraza Lope 2014 *Kukulkan's Realm: Urban Life at Ancient Mayapan*. Boulder: University Press of Colorado.

Menchu, Rigoberta 1984 *I, Rigoberta Menchu: An Indian Woman in Guatemala*. London: Verso.

Meyers, Allan 2005 Material Expressions of Social Inequality on a Porfirian Hacienda in Yucatan, Mexico. *Historical Archaeology* 39(4):112–137.

Miller, Mary, and Simon Martin 2004 *Courtly Art of the Ancient Maya*. San Francisco, CA: Fine Arts Museum of San Francisco.

Mooney, Carolyn 1996 Modern Maya Learn to Decipher Their Ancestors' Hieroglyphics. *The Chronicle of Higher Education*, November 22, 43, 13; B2.

Morehart, Christopher, David Lentz, and Keith Prufer 2005 Wood of the Gods: The Ritual Use of Pine (*Pinus* spp.) by the Ancient Lowland Maya. *Latin American Antiquity* 16(3):255–274.

Prufer, Keith, and James Brady, eds. 2005 *Stone Houses and Earth Lords: Maya Religion in the Cave Context*. Boulder: University Press of Colorado.

Re Cruz, Alicia 1996 *The Two Milpas of Chan Kom*. Albany: State University of New York Press.

Restall, Matthew 2004 Maya Ethnogenesis. *The Journal of Latin American Anthropology* 9(1):64–89.

2009 *The Black Middle: Africans, Mayas, and Spaniards, in Colonial Yucatan*. Stanford, CA: Stanford University Press.

Restall, Matthew, and Amara Solari 2020 *The Maya: A Very Short Introduction*. Oxford: Oxford University Press.

Restall, Matthew, Amara Solari, John Chuchiak, and Traci Ardren 2023 *The Friar and the Maya: Diego de Landa's Account of the Things of Yucatan*. Boulder: University Press of Colorado.

Rissolo, Dominique 2020 In the Realm of Rain Gods: A Contextual Survey of Rock Art across the Northern Maya Lowlands. *Heritage* 3(4):1094–1108.

Saturno, William, David Stuart, Anthony F. Aveni, and Franco Rossi 2012 Ancient Maya Astronomical Tables from Xultun, Guatemala. *Science* 336:714–717.

Scarborough, Vernon L., and David R. Wilcox, eds. 1991 *The Mesoamerican Ballgame*. Tucson: University of Arizona Press.

Seinfeld, Daniel M. 2018 Intoxication Rituals and Gender among the Ancient Maya. In *Ancient Psychoactive Substances*, ed. Scott M. Fitzpatrick, pp. 176–195. Gainesville: University Press of Florida.

Sheets, Payson 2006 *The Ceren Site: An Ancient Village Buried by Volcanic Ash in Central America*. Belmont, CA: Thompson Wadsworth.

Spenard, Jon, Adam King, Terry G. Powis, and Nilesh Gaikwad 2020 A Toast to the Earth: The Social Role of Beverages in Pre-Hispanic Maya Cave Ritual at Pacbitun, Belize. In *Her Cup for Sweet Cacao: Food in Ancient Maya Society*, ed. T. Ardren, pp. 47–86. Austin: University of Texas Press.

Stuart, David 2014 The Chocolatier's Dog. Maya Decipherment, decipherment.wordpress.com/2014/03/26/the-chocolatiers-dog.

Stuart, David, and George Stuart 2008 *Palenque: Eternal City of the Maya*. New York: Thames and Hudson.

Talbot, David 2015 *The Devil's Chessboard: Allan Dulles, the CIA, and the Rise of America's Secret Government*. New York: Harper Collins.

Taube, Karl 2003 Ancient and Contemporary Maya Conceptions about Field and Forest. In *The Lowland Maya Area: Three Millennia at the Human-Wildland Interface*, ed. A. Gomez-Pompa et al., pp. 461–492. New York: Food Products Press.

Thornton, Erin K., Kitty F. Emery, David W. Steadman, Camilla Speller, Ray Matheny, and Dongya Yang 2012 Earliest Mexican Turkeys (*Meleagris gallopavo*) in the Maya Region: Implications for Pre-Hispanic Animal Trade and the Timing of Turkey Domestication. *PLoS One* 7(8):1–8.

Tiesler, Vera 2011 Becoming Maya: Infancy and Upbringing through the Lens of Pre-Hispanic Head Shaping. *Childhood in the Past* 4:117–132.

Tiesler, Vera, Andrea Cucina, Thelma Sierra, Marlene Fall, and Richard Meindl 2005 Comercio, dinámicas biosociales y estructura poblacional del asentimiento costero de Xcambo, Yucatan. *Los Investigadores de la Cultura Maya* 13:365–372.

Tiesler, Vera, Andrea Cucina, Travis W. Stanton, and David A. Freidel 2017 *Before Kukulkan: Bioarchaeology of Maya Life, Death, and Identity and Classic Period Yaxuna*. Tucson: University of Arizona Press.

Tokovinine, Alexandre, and Dmitri Beliaev 2013 People of the Road: Traders and Travelers in Ancient Maya Words and Images. In *Merchants, Markets, and Exchange in the Pre-Columbian World*, eds. Kenneth Hirth and Joanne Pillsbury, pp. 169–200. Washington, DC: Dumbarton Oaks Research Library and Collection.

Vail, Gabrielle, and Maia Dedrick 2020 Human-Deity Relationships Conveyed through Balche' Rituals and Resource Procurement. In *Her Cup for Cacao: Food in Ancient Maya Society*, ed. T. Ardren, pp. 334–365. Austin: University of Texas Press.

Vail, Gabrielle, and Christine Hernandez 2013 *Re-Creating Primordial Time: Foundation Rituals and Mythology in the Postclassic Maya Codices*. Boulder: University Press of Colorado.

Ventura, Carol 2003 The Jakaltek Maya Blowgun in Mythological and Historical Context. *Ancient Mesoamerica* 14(2003):257–268.

Witschey, Walter 1988 Recent Investigations at the Maya Inland Port City of Muyil (Chunyaxche), Quintana Roo, Mexico. *Mexicon* 10(6):111–117.

2005 Muyil: An Early Start and a Late Finish in East Coast Settlement. In *Quintana Roo Archaeology*, eds. J. M. Shaw and J. P. Mathews, pp. 127–143. Tucson: University of Arizona Press.

Index

Everyday Life in the Classic Maya World by Traci Ardren

achiote, 30, 32
agave, 26, 30, 35–37, 53
Aguilar, Geronimo de, 151
alcohol, alcoholic substances, 28, 30, 57, 103, 110
almanac, 35, 53, 95, 112, 122 *see* codices
ancestors, 78, 83, 86, 92, 96, 98–99, 101–103, 130, 146, 150, 158
ancestral, 16, 32, 86, 88, 97, 109, 142
apiculture (beekeeping), 22, 56, 59, 159
apprenticeship, 34
artisans, artists 74, 80, 82–83, 94, 106, 111, 118, 156, 160–161 (*see also* craftspeople)
astronomy, 20, 83–84, 116, 119, 120–121
avocado, 30, 32, 66, 74
axis mundi, 27
Aztec, 14, 16, 25, 41, 114, 127, 136, 150–152

backstrap loom 36, 115, (*see also* weaving)
Balancanche Cave, 66
balche, 28, 30, 57–58, 66
ball game, 22, 89–93, 109
ball player, 39, 85, 91–92
beans, 16, 30, 31, 40, 43, 53–56, 60, 74, 77, 88, 109–110, 112, 131, 141, 146, 149, 159

bees, 30, 46, 56–59, 68, 159
bee products (*see* honey)
beekeeping 22, 160 (*see* apiculture)
beeswax, 39–40, 46, 56–58, 72, 75, 84, 115, 153
Bonampak 138

cacao, 12, 16, 73–74, 77, 109–110, 138, 140–141, 151
Calakmul, 3, 86, 94, 106, 141
calendar, 2, 16, 20, 22, 78–79, 83–84, 91, 102, 104, 117, 119–122, 156
canoes, 23, 125–127, 129–131, 133–137, 139, 142, 144, 151–152
captives, 20, 41, 86–88, 99
Caracol, 17
caves, 20, 42, 49, 64–66, 68, 117, 135
ceiba, 30–32, 66, 115
cenote, 11, 65
ceramics, 4, 6, 18, 25, 27–29, 32–39, 49, 57, 59, 62, 66, 74, 77–78, 82–83, 87, 92, 103, 105, 108–109, 115–116, 121, 133, 135, 137–138, 151
Ceren, 67
Chac, 11, 49
chaya, 30–31
chert, 37, 61, 133
Chichen Itza, 149–150

169

chicle, 126
child, 43, 46, 85, 90, 107
　children, 2, 5, 21, 25, 27, 31, 34, 36–38, 40–41, 72, 89, 98, 101–102, 106, 118, 143
Chi, Gaspar Antonio, 153
chili peppers, 3, 12, 25, 30, 32, 110
Chunchucmil, 26, 132, 138
Central Intelligence Agency (CIA), 155
Classic period, 1, 3–5, 11–16, 20–23, 29, 33, 35, 37, 39–41, 46–47, 52, 55–57, 61–63, 67, 69–70, 74, 76–77, 81–83, 85–86, 88, 90, 93–96, 101–110, 112–113, 116–118, 121–122, 124–125, 127, 129–132, 134–141, 144, 147–150, 152–153, 157–161
cloth, 5, 30, 32, 36, 47, 57, 88, 94, 99, 109, 115, 126, 137, 141, 151
　cotton, 36, 88, 90, 94, 109, 115, 136–137, 151
　other plant fibers, 30, 35–37, 76, 115, 134, 140
Coba, 20, 27, 27, 37, 55, 64, 70–71, 74–76, 78, 91, 100, 126–128, 140, 161
codices, 35, 53, 95, 119
Columbus, Christopher, 12, 151
complementarity, 47
conch, 62, 112, 117, 131, 134
cooking, 25, 27, 31, 34, 40, 44, 94, 115
corn, 11, 18–19, 26, 44, 46–50, 52–57, 59, 60, 63, 65, 67, 73–74, 81, 84–85, 88, 90, 95, 100, 107, 110–112, 114–115, 117, 121, 124–126, 130–131, 135, 139–140, 144, 146, 149, 157, 159–160
　cornfield, 11, 21, 23, 31, 34, 40, 46, 48–49, 53, 55–57, 59–60, 63, 70–71, 73, 85, 91, 126, 146
Cortes, Hernando, 12, 151
cotton, 26, 30, 35, 36, 88, 90, 94, 96, 108–109, 115, 136–137, 139, 151, 153

Cozumel, 135, 151–152
craft, 22, 34–35, 94, 113, 121
　crafting, 21, 34
　craft workshops, 34
　craftspeople 2, 16, 34, 39, 70, 74, 124
creator deities, 17, 58, 115, 137
currency, 77

dancers, dancing 48, 77, 99, 111–112, 144
descendant communities 157, 158
deer 12, 29–30, 59–62, 109, 127, 145
deities, 4, 11, 15–18, 28, 46, 48–49, 52, 61, 65–68, 74, 122, 125–126
　see specific
diplomacy 79, 95
dogs 60, 62–63, 143, 164
domestic life 21, 40
domestication 46, 72, 164, 167–168
dragon fruit 30
drought 11, 56, 92, 150
duck 12, 28–29, 40, 60, 125, 134

enslaved people 41–42, 95
entheogens 103

farmers, farming 4, 13–14, 16, 21, 46, 49, 52–53, 55–57, 63, 67, 69–70, 72, 85, 93, 124, 149, 151–152, 160, 165–167
feasting 99, 122
fertilizer 29, 52, 55
figurines 4, 5, 37, 40, 45, 97, 136
fish 9, 12, 55, 61, 74, 125, 129, 132–136, 146, 166
flowers 30, 56, 59, 115
food, foodways 2, 4, 7, 12–13, 25, 27, 35, 37–39, 41–42, 44, 46–47, 49, 55–57, 59–61, 65, 68–69, 76, 93–94, 98, 104, 108–109, 111–115, 121, 132, 134, 142–143, 145, 148, 153, 155, 158, 163–164, 168

Index

forest 22, 24, 26, 37–38, 40, 46–47, 49–53, 55–57, 59–61, 63, 65–68, 72, 96–97, 99, 101, 127, 129, 143, 151, 165, 168
Franciscan 104, 152, 154
fruit 12, 25, 29–32, 44, 49, 63, 66, 76, 95, 125, 156 (see var kinds)

gardens 3, 21, 25, 27–30, 35–36, 41, 55, 71, 73
  household 4–5, 12, 20, 27, 29, 30, 33–36, 41–42, 45, 47–48, 55, 60, 70, 74, 85, 99, 112, 125, 140–141, 165
  gardening 21, 25
gender 4–5, 11, 18, 21, 45, 47–48, 64, 115, 125, 136, 148, 164–165, 167
graffiti 79, 118–119
guava 12, 29, 42
Guerrero, Gonzalo 152

hair, hair treatment 37, 40, 47–48, 74, 76, 117, 143
hematite 33, 79, 144
heritage 148, 155, 157–158, 161, 163, 167
  archaeological 5–6, 8, 17, 21, 35, 53, 67, 109, 112, 142, 149, 157–158, 162, 166
  culinary 29, 158, 163
Hero Twins 18, 47, 59, 61, 90, 139, 161
hieroglyphic inscriptions 4, 67, 70, 94, 108, 118
highlands 7, 9, 11, 39, 55, 75–76, 79, 84–85, 113, 115, 124, 135, 140–141, 154, 156, 161
hip-hop 147, 161–163
honey, 12, 46, 56–59, 75, 110–111, 131, 159
huipil 40

Isla Cerritos 131, 163
Itzamna 58, 138

jade 9, 16, 27, 33, 40–41, 48, 75, 101, 113–115, 121, 136, 141, 143–145, 153, 166
  jade net skirt 48
jaguars 7, 37, 59, 127
javelina 60
Juun Ixim (One Maize) 47–48

La Corona 72, 106
Landa, Bishop Diego de 25, 57, 104
learning 4–5, 15, 40, 53, 55, 111, 118, 125, 147
loincloths 36, 48, 138

maize 4, 11–12, 18–19, 22, 25–27, 29, 31, 37–38, 44, 46–50, 52–57, 59–60, 63, 65, 67, 73–74, 81, 84–85, 88, 90, 95, 100, 107, 110–112, 114–115, 117, 121, 124–126, 131–132, 136, 140–141, 145, 147, 150, 158, 160–162, 164, 167 (see corn)
Maize Deity 11, 18, 47–48, 81, 90, 100, 107, 117, 121
Malintzin (La Malinche) 153, 166
manioc 55
mano and metate 25, 110, 158
markets, marketplace 13, 22–24, 70, 77–78, 85, 93, 146, 166, 168
marriage 25, 48, 89, 101–102, 104–107
marriage alliance 101–102, 106
math, mathematics 20, 83, 119, 120, 146, 168
Maya "'collapse'" 14, 148, 149
Mayan language 4, 15, 147, 153, 161–163
Mayapan 151, 167
medicine, medicinal 30, 40, 52, 57, 66, 68, 72
Menchu, Rigoberto 156, 167
merchants 3–4, 137–139, 145–146, 149, 151, 168
midden 60, 132
midwives, midwifery 42–43

monkeys 59, 61, 81, 96
Moon goddess 29, 107
murals 112, 117, 142, 151
music, musical instruments 112, 161, 162
Muyil 128–130, 146, 168

Nahua language, 25
Naranjo 105
night 27, 29, 41, 44, 59, 60, 66, 77, 89, 95–98, 104, 112, 143
nixtamal 25

obsidian 4, 9, 27, 35, 37, 61, 75–76, 99, 134, 138, 140–141, 143, 161
ocarina 40
offerings 16, 32, 34, 49–51, 65–66, 68, 136

palaces 2, 22, 24, 37, 70, 79, 83, 88, 93, 94, 106, 109, 115, 118, 147, 150–151, 162
Palenque 18, 19, 66, 163, 165, 168
passionfruit 30
patolli 43–45, 85
Paynes Creek 134, 166
peccary 12, 59–61, 63, 75, 127
plant fibers 35–37, 76, 135, 141
polygyny 106
Postclassic period 12, 14, 41, 87, 93, 117, 128, 130, 148–152, 168
pozole 25, 31, 38, 49, 95
Preclassic period 12–13, 117, 120, 130, 142, 148, 165
pyramids 3, 7, 13, 20–21, 65, 71, 73, 78–79, 151
pyrite 75, 121

queen 16, 20–21, 29, 33, 43, 57, 60, 72, 77, 80–81, 86, 88–89, 95, 97, 99, 101–103, 105–106, 111–112, 123, 143, 145, 165
Queen K'awiil Ajaw 20–21, 97, 100

rain 9, 11, 24, 44, 46–47, 49, 52–53, 58–59, 63, 65–66, 68, 92, 167

ramon 31, 74
rejolladas 73
rituals 11, 13, 15, 18, 21, 24, 29, 30, 40, 43, 45, 47, 50, 65, 67–68, 80, 85, 88, 97–99, 102, 105, 111, 117, 120–121, 145, 154, 163, 167, 168
funerary 20, 79
hunting 18, 22, 60–63, 135
inauguration 78, 99
roads 21, 71, 73, 79, 93, 129

salt 77, 125, 128, 134–135, 140–143, 145–146, 163, 166
San Bartolo 117
Santa Barbara 133
sapodilla 29
scribes 19–20, 22, 35, 70, 81–84, 89, 104, 116–118, 120, 122
sea 19, 22, 48, 124–125, 127, 129, 130–132, 134, 136, 141, 143–145
shell, shell ornaments 9, 17, 34, 37, 40, 48, 62, 74, 91, 94, 112–113, 117, 121, 128, 135–137, 143–144
shrines 16, 45, 136, 151
spondylus 48, 113, 137, 143–144
squash 12, 53–56, 60, 65, 74, 147, 150
stelae 21, 48, 80, 83–86, 101, 106, 118, 123, 128, 150, 165
Sun god 29
sweatbaths 43, 65–67, 165

tamales 25, 31, 41, 43, 49, 55, 75–76, 111–112
tapir 56, 59, 61, 63, 95–96
tattoos 37, 40, 76
temples 11, 18–19, 24, 50, 65, 70, 74, 77–80, 85, 93, 97, 99, 117, 120, 128–129, 131, 137, 151 (*see also* shrines)
Terminal Classic period 13, 25, 150–151
terraces 55–56, 94

Index

three Sisters 54–55
three stone hearth 27
Tikal 86, 119
Tonina 110
tortilla 25, 158
tourism 149, 158, 162–163
trade 13–14, 22, 40, 57, 72–76, 85,
  110, 112, 124–125, 130, 132,
  137–142, 144–146, 151, 153,
  163, 168
 maritime 22, 130, 151
 traders 22–23, 72, 74–77, 108,
  124, 128, 130–132, 137–143,
  145–146, 152, 168
travel 1, 5, 22, 27, 49, 72–73, 75,
  130–131, 136, 143, 145, 158,
  160, 162
 canoe 125–126, 128, 131–132,
  135–138, 143, 152, 166
tree crops 73
tree islands 127
tribute 21, 35, 37, 49, 73, 88, 105,
  108–110, 112, 137, 151
Tulum 15, 128
turkey 12, 28–29, 31, 44, 60,
  109–110, 142–143, 168
tzolkin 84–85, *see* calendar

underworld 2, 18–19, 30, 33, 44, 61,
  63, 65, 90, 92, 125, 131,
  138–139, 144
United Fruit Company 156
urbanism 69, 122, 151, 163–165

Venus 44, 84–85, 98, 120

walls, boundary 13, 22, 24, 26, 49,
  55, 67, 73–74, 91, 103,
  108–109, 116–119, 121, 125,
  131, 135, 145
wahy 43, 95–96
Waka (El Peru) 74
warriors 74, 85–86, 88, 153, 161,
  165
water, water management 9, 12,
  19, 20, 25, 27–29, 32, 37–40,
  44, 47, 49, 55–57, 61,
  63–68, 73–74, 79, 95, 97, 110,
  125, 127–132, 134–136,
  141, 143, 145–146, 153, 163,
  166
weaving, 25, 36, 76
wells 27–28, 63, 73, 79, 127, 136,
  150
workshops, craft 22, 35, 40, 94, 113,
  121, 135, 158–159

Xcambo 134, 168
Xcaret 128
Xuenkal 6, 34, 48, 128
Xultun 83, 116, 164, 167

Yalahau 130, 165
Yaxchilan 88, 106
Yaxunah 5, 7, 58, 157–158, 163

zapote 25, 29